GROWTH

① **GOODNESS · TRUTH · PERFECTION · CLARITY · JUSTICE · SELF CONTROL**

1

② **HELPFULNESS · ALTRUISM · LOVING · BOLD · SERVANTS HEART · DISCERNING NEEDS**

2

③ **EFFICIENCY · ACTION · ENCOURAGER · ESTABLISHER · INSPIRING · EXCELLENCE**

3

④ **CREATIVITY · EMPATHY · LOVE OF BEAUTY · SPACE SAVER · EMOTIONALLY HONEST**

4

⑤ **VISION · STEADFASTNESS · CLARITY · FAITHFULNESS · HUMILITY · WISDOM**

5

⑥ **COURAGE · GUARDIANSHIP · KINDNESS · LOYALTY · STRENGTH · FAITHFULNESS**

6

⑦ **SPONTANEITY · JOY · THANKFULNESS · HOPE · LONG SUFFERING · VISION**

7

⑧ **STRENGTH · ZEAL · VIGILANT · ZEALOUS · PROTECTOR · TENDERNESS**

8

⑨ **PEACE · KINDNESS · EMPATHY · PATIENCE · GENTLENESS · UNDERSTANDING**

9

Through her beautifully articulate words, Elisabeth accurately portrays the shadow side of each Enneagram type while also highlighting the rich grace and freedom found in the spiritual journey of integration. Pairing Scripture with reflection questions and prayers, the devotions help guide the reader on the pathway of personal and spiritual growth in a powerful way that is unique to their type.

—*Meredith Boggs*
The Other Half Podcast

If you know your Enneagram type and you're ready to make meaningful steps toward growth, this book is for you. Elisabeth combines her Enneagram expertise with her deep faith to guide readers toward self-understanding, growth, and transformation through contemplative yet practical writing. This devotional is a great tool that you'll return to again and again.

—*Steph Barron Hall*
Nine Types Co.
Enneagram writer, coach, and teacher

the
HELPER

GROWING AS AN ENNEAGRAM

60-DAY ENNEAGRAM DEVOTIONAL

the
HELPER

GROWING AS AN ENNEAGRAM

2

ELISABETH BENNETT

W

WHITAKER
HOUSE

Introduction images created by Katherine Waddell.

THE HELPER
Growing as an Enneagram 2

Elisabethbennettenneagram.com
Instagram: @Enneagram.Life
Facebook.com/enneagramlife

ISBN: 978-1-64123-507-5
eBook ISBN: 978-1-64123-508-2
Printed in the United States of America
© 2020 by Elisabeth Bennett

Whitaker House
1030 Hunt Valley Circle
New Kensington, PA 15068
www.whitakerhouse.com

Library of Congress Cataloging-in-Publication Data (Pending)

1 2 3 4 5 6 7 8 9 10 11 **Ⱳ** 27 26 25 24 23 22 21 20

Dedication

To all the Twos holding this book, you are wanted, deeply adored, and whole in the eyes of our heavenly Father.

Contents

Foreword

I first learned about the Enneagram about five years ago. I was traveling in the Holy Land with twenty-five other women and remember hearing many of them say things like, "I'm an Eight" and "What's your wing?" I was intrigued to know what they were talking about, but when I asked, the brief explanation they offered was mostly confusing. Once back in the States, I went online and found an Enneagram test. I took it and tied for a Two and a Seven. This meant very little to me, so I texted some of the women from the trip and shared my results. One of my friends, who had been familiar with and practicing Enneagram work for most of her adult life, said to me, "I think you are most definitely a Two."

Over the next two years, the Enneagram went from a strange and curious *personality test* very few people I knew had ever heard of, to a more well-known and accepted personality typology. And today, the Enneagram is widely known and wildly popular, so much so that questions such as, "What's your number?" now refers to one's Enneagram number and not one's phone number.

My personal Enneagram journey began to take root right around the time the Enneagram began to show up in more and more spaces. I learned that the test I took would only shed a sliver of light on my number and that I needed to dive much deeper to gain the understanding and self-awareness I was craving. So, I started reading books such as *The Road Back to You* by Ian Cron and Suzanne Stabile. I began listening to Enneagram specific podcasts, searching for episodes about Twos. And the more I learned, the more the number resonated with me. It was as though a spotlight was shining on my soul.

It was also around this time that I had my first experience with being totally rejected by a dear friend. It was a rejection that wounded me deeply; I felt shocked, confused, and ashamed, wondering why I couldn't just *get over it* and move on. As I look back on this time, I can see God's grace. The work I was doing with the Enneagram gave me more self-awareness than I ever had before. I was beginning to understand, as it played out in real-time, that this broken friendship devastated me because it was the manifestation of my greatest fear: to be unwanted.

Almost three years later, it still pains me that this person and I are not friends. When I see her on social media, I still feel a tinge of pain as I remember the ways she shut me out of her life. But instead of thinking I am too sensitive or feeling embarrassed by my feelings, I have a better understanding and more self-awareness. I realize that as a Two, I am intrinsically motivated by my desire to feel loved and be needed. I can look back now and see that when I was living without the Enneagram self-awareness, that my motivation for love, when not fostered in a healthy way, may have been the very thing that caused this friend to reject me.

The thing I love the most about this devotional is that no matter where you are with your understanding of the Enneagram, this is a tool to do the very thing I needed help with years ago, a tool that offers us a deeper perception that we can turn into practical transformation. May these next sixty days mold you and shape you into the Two God created you to be.

—Heather Avis, Author
The Lucky Few: Finding God's Best in the Most Unlikely Places and *Scoot Over and Make Some Room: Creating a Space Where Everyone Belongs*

Acknowledgments

My journey from young hopeful writer, all the way back to the tender age of four, to holding books with my name on them hasn't been easy or pretty. In fact, it's held a lot of hurt, disappointment, and rejection. However, as you hold a book with my name on the cover in your hands, I'd love you to know who and what has sustained me through it all. You are holding a piece of God's redemption in my story, tangible proof of His kindness, and testament of His faithfulness. I didn't break any doors down, or *do* anything myself that ensured my trajectory of publishing. God in His kindness handed me this opportunity, and to Him alone belongs all the glory and praise.

My agent, Amanda, deserves the highest of thanks and admiration. Thank you for answering my many questions, guiding, and giving me the confidence to do this. I couldn't have done it without you. To all the people at Whitaker House, my editor, Peg, and publisher, Christine, thank you for making these devotionals what they are today. It's been a pleasure working with you all.

To my writing community hope*writers, thank you for giving me the courage to call myself a writer long before I felt like one. To Alison Bradley whose heart and words for the Twos reading this devotional are so timely and beautiful. Thank you for pouring your heart and soul into this book. To Heather Avis, whose heart for her fellow Twos can be felt through her beautiful foreword, thank you for being one of the first pair of eyes on this book. You are truly an amazing example of a protective, deeply caring, and fierce advocate Two. Thank you to Pastor Bubba Jennings at Resurrection Church for reading over my proposal and giving me advice on how to serve Jesus well in this process.

The people who have been the biggest support and help to me during this process, and if I'm honest, my life, are:

Christine Rollings, thank you so much for how you have loved your fellow Twos through your writing in this devotional. I know that wading through the depths of your inner thoughts and behaviors can be so taxing, but you did it as a labor of love. Thank you for being a kind "me too" to the Twos who are reading this. You were a pleasure to work with.

To all the Twos who have helped me not only learn about your type in a deeper way, but also inspired so many of the words in this devotional: Madeline Smith, Kathryn Coffman, Suzanne Stabile, Heather Avis, all my type Two clients, and a couple other suspected Twos that I won't publicly *type* here. Thank you!

Sarah Upton, thank you for faithfully helping with Wellington during this entire journey. I am so comfortable when he is with you, and I adore how much you love him.

Mikayla Larson, thank you for your friendship, support, and for being here when I've needed you the most. You are such a gift in my life.

John and Jan Bennett, thank you for faithfully praying for me and supporting me through this entire process. Your encouragement has moved mountains and sustained me on the hardest days.

Thank you, Mom and Dad (Joe and Diane Upton), for literally teaching me to read and write, and encouraging me to say yes to big things. I would never have had the foundation to say yes without you, and how you raised me. I'm so proud and grateful to have the two of you in my corner cheering me on.

Peter, you've been beyond supporting, patient, and caring towards me. You have taught me so much about what it means to be faithful, and you never let me quit. You believe in me enough for both of us, and I can't believe the gift that you are in my life. You're my best friend and I love you.

Introduction
What Is the Enneagram?

The Enneagram is an ancient personality typology for which no one really knows the origins.

It uses nine points within a circle—the word itself means "a drawing of nine"—to represent nine distinct personality types. The points are numbered simply to differentiate between them, with each point having no greater or less value than the others. The theory is that a person assumes one of these personalities in childhood as a reaction to discovering the world as a scary, unkind place and thus, unlikely to accept his or her true self.

The nine types are identified by their numbers or by these names:

1. The Perfectionist
2. The Helper
3. The Achiever
4. The Individualist
5. The Thinker
6. The Guardian
7. The Enthusiast
8. The Challenger
9. The Peacemaker

HOW DO I FIND MY TYPE?

Your Enneagram type is determined by your main motivation. Finding your Enneagram type is a journey, as we are typically unaware of our motivations and instead focus on our behaviors. Many online tests focus around behaviors, and while some motivations *may* produce certain behaviors, that may not always be the case and you are unlikely to get accurate results.

To find your Enneagram type, you need to start by learning about *all* nine Enneagram types, and explore their motivations in contrast to your own behaviors and deeper motivations.

You can ask for feedback from those around you, but most often, the more you learn, the clearer your core number shines through.

It's often the number whose description makes you feel the most *exposed* that is your true core type. Your core Enneagram number won't change, since it's solidified in childhood.

Each number's distinct motivation:

1. Integrity – Goodness
2. Love – Relationships
3. Worth – Self-Importance
4. Authenticity – Unique Identity
5. Competency – Objective Truth
6. Security – Guidance
7. Satisfaction – Freedom
8. Independence – Control
9. Peace – Equilibrium

IS THIS JOURNEY WORTH IT?

Yes! The self-awareness you gain along the way is gold, and learning about the other types in the process brings you so much empathy and understanding for all of the other personalities in your life.

WHAT MAKES THE ENNEAGRAM UNIQUE AND DIFFERENT FROM MYERS-BRIGGS, STRENGTHSFINDER, OR DISC ASSESSMENTS?

The Enneagram, unlike other typology systems, is fluid. Yes, the Enneagram tells you what your base personality characteristics are, but it also reveals how you change when you're growing, stressed, secure, unhealthy, healthy, etc.

You are not the same person at twenty as you are at sixty. You're not the same person at your stressful workplace as you are when binge-watching your favorite TV show and eating ice cream at home. The Enneagram accounts for these inconsistencies and changes in your behavior and informs you of when or how those changes occur.

If you look at the following graph, you'll see that each of the numbers connects to two other numbers by arrows. The arrow pointed toward your number is your growth arrow; the arrow pointed away is your stress number. When your life leaves you with more room to breathe, you exhibit positive characteristics of your growth number, and when you're stretched thin in seasons of stress, you exhibit the negative characteristics of your stress number.

This is one explanation for big shifts in personality over a lifetime.

Another point of difference between the Enneagram and other typology systems is *wings*. Your wings are the two numbers on either side of your core number, which add flavor to your personality type. Although your core number won't change—and your main motivation, sin proclivities, and personality—will come from that core number, your wings can be very influential on your overall personality and how it presents itself. There are many different theories about wings, but the viewpoint we hold to is:

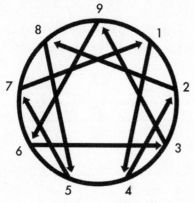

1. Your wing can only be one of the two numbers on either side of your number. Therefore, you can be a 2 with a 1 wing (2w1) but not a 2 with a 5 wing (2w5).

2. You have access to the numbers on either side of your number, but most people will only have one dominant wing. (*Dominant* meaning you exhibit more of the behaviors of one wing than the other wing.) It is possible to have equal wings or no wing at all, but this is rare.

3. Your dominant wing number can change from one to the other throughout your life, but it's speculated this might only happen once.

As you read through this book, we will go over what an Enneagram Two looks like with both of its wings. If you're struggling to figure out what your core number is, this book series could really help give you some more in-depth options!

HOW DO YOU BECOME YOUR TYPE?

Personality is a kind of shield we pick up and hide behind. It is functional, even protective at times, but altogether unnecessary because God made us in His image from the start. However, we cling to this personality like it's our key to survival, and nothing has proven us wrong so far. It's the only tool we've ever had, and the shield has scratches and dents to prove its worth.

Not all parts of our personality are wrong or bad, but by living in a fallen, sinful world, we all tend to distort even good things in bad ways. Amen?

What personality did you pick up in childhood? If you're reading this devotional, then you may have chosen type Two. You chose your shield because your need to be loved became the one thing that your life revolved around from early childhood until right now, at this very moment. The Enneagram talks about childhood wounds and how we pick up a particular shield as a reaction to these wounds. However, not all siblings have the same Enneagram type even though they heard the same wounding message or had the same harmful experiences growing up. This is because we are born with our own unique outlook on the world, and we filter everything through that outlook. You and your siblings may have heard the same things, but while you heard, "You're only loved when there's no conflict in your life," your sibling heard, "You're only loved when you're successful." Thus, you both would become different Enneagram types.

Trauma and abuse of any kind can definitely impact your choice of shield as well. If you think of all these nine shields as being a different color, perhaps you were born predisposed to be more likely to pick blue than red. However, in a moment of early trauma, you might have heard someone shouting, "Pick black! Black is the only option!" Thus, you chose black instead of blue, which would've been your own unique reaction to your life circumstances. It's hard to say how these things happen exactly, especially when trauma is involved. Are you who you are *despite* trauma...or because of it? Only God knows, but there is healing and growth to be found either way.

We've all heard the phrase, "You can't teach an old dog new tricks." I'd like to propose that when referencing personality, it might be said, "The longer you use your personality, the harder it is to see its ineffectiveness." It's not impossible for an older person to drastically change for the better, but it will be harder for them to put down what has worked for them for so long. That's why, as we age, it can become harder to even see where our personality ends and our true self begins. Even if the unhealthy parts of our personality have been ineffective, they still seem to be the only things that have worked for us.

WHY DO WE NEED THE ENNEAGRAM WHEN WE HAVE THE HOLY SPIRIT AND THE BIBLE TO GUIDE US?

The Enneagram is a helpful tool, but only when it is used as such. The Enneagram cannot save you—only Jesus can do that.

However, God made us all unique, and we all reflect Him in individual ways. Learning about these unique reflections can encourage us, as well as point us toward our purposes. The Enneagram also reveals the sin problems and blind spots you may unknowingly struggle with. Revealing these blind spots leads us to repentance and change before God.

HOW DO I CHANGE MY MORE NEGATIVE BEHAVIORS?

Alcoholics Anonymous was really on to something when they called their first step "admitting you have a problem." How do you solve a problem if you don't know you have one or are in denial about it? You can't. If you have a shield you're using to protect yourself from the world, but are blissfully unaware of its existence, you won't understand how its very existence impacts you and your relationships. You definitely won't be putting that battered but battle-tested shield of a personality down anytime soon.

Similar to the wisdom of admitting one has a problem before recovery can begin, the Enneagram proposes self-knowledge as the starting point before there can be change.

Whether you're 100 percent sure you are a Two, or just curious about the possibility, this is what it looks like to be a Two.

What It Means to Be a Helper

Enneagrams Twos are traditionally called "the Helpers," and if you're a Two, you probably understand why. You're drawn toward helping; it's probably one of the things you like best about yourself, and others seem to appreciate it too.

The Helper has an ability to foresee needs like no one else, and they love meeting needs and looking for all the little ways they can be helpful. When healthy, Helpers are generous, kind, sure of themselves, and empathetic. When unhealthy, they can be possessive of their loved ones, manipulative, and angry when criticized.

Christine, who you'll hear from later in this book, has a very typical Helper story. Even in her childhood, Christine mothered. Not only was she the oldest child, but she was the oldest girl of four children, putting her in the role of *second mom*. Christine fell into this role with ease, and enjoyed the responsibility that came with helping her Mom and keeping her siblings alive. What this didn't leave much room for was Christine herself. *Mom is busy, I need to help her*, and *My needs are a burden* were thoughts that Christine subconsciously accepted as facts.

As a single young woman, Christine felt an overwhelming desire for a relationship. In her most vulnerable I-don't-like-being-single prayers with God, she'd cry, "I just have so much love to give!"

Even after she was married, this cry followed her as she struggled to get pregnant with her first child. The ache to love, nurture, and develop loving relationships felt all-consuming. "I'm so ready for this!"

Now, as she holds, feeds, and cares for the needs of her new-born daughter, Christine feels at home. Being needed feels like love, being in sync with her daughter's needs and fulfilling them feels productive, and having someone who depends fully on her gives her a great sense of worth. She loves her daughter dearly. In the back of her mind, she is thrilled at the thought of this great love being returned to her by her daughter someday. "Mama, I love you." Won't those be wonderful words?

Enneagram Twos are naturals at nurturing, and even though Christine is a woman, the oldest daughter, and a mom, men also make very nurturing Twos. A single male Two may struggle with this concept of being nurturing, but if he really takes a hard look at his life, he'll find this strength alive and well. Nurturing can look like bringing a meal to a sick friend, being a kind and empathetic leader, or seeing the best in someone and cheering them on. There are so many ways Twos nurture and love people outside of parenthood.

As parents, Twos are in their element. Twos as parents look near to perfection. They sacrifice their needs for their children and can anticipate these needs; there seems to be no end to their nurturing love. This looks so perfect because Twos are motivated by love. It's even theorized that Twos think about relationships 80 percent of the time.

Are Twos the perfect Enneagram number? Before you rip this page out, hang it in your house, and make copies to send to all your friends, I have to tell you that Twos' strength can also be their greatest weakness. When a Two's children grow up, they may believe that payment is due for their daily loving sacrifice. This sneaks up on the Two as much as it does on their children, as Twos are often very unaware of their expectations for their children. These expectations may sound like, "My children would do anything for me," "My children will love me," "My children will dote on me," and "My children think I'm the best mother ever." These are secret expectations Twos can put on their children as they grow up.

What tragically happens (I've seen this more than once) is that Twos demand payment for all their years of sacrifice, and their children get confused by this change. Instead of bending to the needs of these parents, the children will often find, befriend, or marry another Two who will fulfill their needs as their parents did.

If Twos can catch these expectation-setting thoughts, and hold them captive in obedience to Christ (see 2 Corinthians 10:5), they can change not only their own destiny but the legacy of their families. How do they do this? Well, only by the changing power of God through the Holy Spirit, but the Enneagram can help. I pray that this devotional will help you understand yourself and how God made you, and that it will draw you near to Him as He lovingly helps you to grow.

All About Being a Two

MOTIVATION

To feel loved and know that those around them feel loved by them; to be needed and esteemed by others as generous or kind

Most people would agree that "All we need is love," but for Twos, love is *everything*. Other types want to be respected, admired, or given freedom, and those things feel like love to them, but Twos want all five love languages every second, all day, all the time. Twos are really good at showing you love because they're very intuitive to others' needs!

BIGGEST FEAR

Being unwanted or unworthy of love

This prompts them to try really hard to be worthy of your love and keep your affection by making themselves indispensable to you.

HEART TRIAD

Each Enneagram type is dominant in either feeling, thinking, or doing. These *triads* are referred to as heart-centered, head-centered, or gut-centered.

Twos, along with Threes and Fours, are part of the heart triad. This means that they first process information as feelings before moving on to thinking or doing. In the most practical sense, others' actions tend to feel very personal, as information is first processed by feeling before it is thought about logically. Those in the heart triad may be told they are too sensitive.

Each of the three triads also has a defining emotion connected to the center they use most.

For the heart triad, this emotion is shame. Twos, Threes, and Fours struggle to believe that they have inherent worth and believe that they must *do* something in order to have worth.

As we know from Scripture, God formed us in the womb of our mother, and He gave us worth. This means that our worth cannot be taken away from us, we cannot earn our worth, and we cannot add more worth to ourselves by doing anything.

> *Look at the birds of the air: they neither sow nor reap nor gather into barns, and yet your heavenly Father feeds them. Are you not of more value than they?*   (Matthew 6:26)

Yes, of course, we are worth more than birds. God made us in His own image, with thoughts, feelings, desires, and dominion here on earth.

> *So God created man in his own image, in the image of God he created him; male and female he created them. And God blessed them. And God said to them, "Be fruitful and multiply and fill the earth and subdue it, and have dominion over the fish of the sea and over the birds of the heavens and over every living thing that moves on the earth.*
>
> (Genesis 1:27–28)

God is the One who gave us worth. The Creator who put breath in our lungs gave us value here on earth. How much time do we waste doubting that value? For those in the heart triad, the answer is a lot!

Shame comes into play when Satan uses the lie "You'll never be worth anything" to paralyze Twos and condemn them. If he cannot destroy you and your future, Satan will try to steal your peace and the good works God has set before you to do.

CHILDHOOD WOUND

The wounding message Twos heard (or thought they heard) as children was, "It is not okay to have your own needs" or "Don't be a burden." These children often felt like their own needs were selfish, and they were only truly loved when they were helping others. This led to a life of frantically putting the needs of others before their own, and becoming increasingly frustrated when they realize their own needs are unmet.

A Two might have heard a parent or guardian saying something like, "Be a good boy/girl and help me," "You're so selfish," "You need to put others before yourself," "You need to help your mom; she needs you," "Don't take/do that; you're being selfish," or "You're so thoughtful! I just love how helpful you are." Getting positive attention only when they *helped* could have been very damaging as well.

THE LOST CHILDHOOD MESSAGE TWOS LONG TO HEAR

"You are wanted."

Even if you have needs, even if you don't help, or even if someone else has to step up to the plate, you're fully wanted and loved by Christ. Not only that, you're fully wanted and loved even when you say no and even when you ask for your needs to be met. You are not too needy for His love.

DEFENSE MECHANISM

Repression is the defense mechanism Twos use when they encounter feelings, desires, or urges that go against their preferred *helpful/you first* behaviors. Repression can be hard to pinpoint in your own life; however, repressed feelings don't just go away without a fight. Repressed feelings often come out sideways as manipulative behaviors, passive aggression, or other "nice" controlling behaviors.

WINGS

As I mentioned earlier, your wings are the numbers on either side of your core number that add flavor to your core number.

Two with a One Wing (2w1)

No one wants to be seen as helpful, dependable, and responsible as much as a Two with a One wing. A One wing will add some emotional awareness to a Two, but coupling it with a more introverted nature can make it hard for them to express those emotions. Seeking to do things for others, and to have fulfilling relationships, a 2w1 will strive for dependability, and often have a hard time saying no. That being said, they make faithful, responsible, and helpful employees, friends, neighbors, and family members. In short, everyone loves a 2w1 and wants them on their team. A One wing can make a Two more critical of themselves, more controlling of their environment, and more prone to carrying the weight of the world on their shoulders. However, a healthy 2w1 will find a healthy balance of boundaries and helpfulness, but it can take a while for them to give themselves any slack for not being the one to do the helping.

Two with a Three Wing (2w3)

A Three wing will add a competitive drive to a Two's natural others-first mentality. They are often more energetic and outgoing than an average Two (or a 2w1). They will use this energy to do more and help more in a way that not many other types could compete with, and that's just the way a 2w3 likes it.

Caring, extroverted, praise-seeking, and a natural conversationalist, a 2w3 can be quite the charmer, and if they are not careful, they can end up using people to gain the admiration their wing type craves.

When healthy, these helpful achievers are wonderful to have at your side, and they have a good grasp on what tasks they should actually help with.

ARROWS

Your arrows are the two numbers your Enneagram number are connected to in the Enneagram diagram. These two arrows represent the number from which you get the best traits as you grow, or the number from which you get the worst traits when you're in seasons of stress.

Stress: Going to Eight

When a Two is in stress, they can take on some of the negative characteristics of an Eight. The normally sweet and giving Twos will become aggressive, argumentative, and even hostile as they react out of the unhealthy side of Eights. It might surprise even the Twos themselves when they lash out and become quite a force to be reckoned with when stressed.

Growth: Going to Four

Twos become more emotionally aware as they start to react to life like a healthy Four. Creative, emotionally honest, and self-nurturing, a secure Two won't need to be fixing someone else's problems to feel fulfilled and worthy.

TYPE TWO SUBTYPES

When we talk about subtypes and the Enneagram, we are referring to three relational instincts we all have. These instincts, like those of *fight or flight*, are reactions over which we have little control. The three relational subtypes are Self-Preservation (Sp), Social (So), and One-to-One (Sx). We all have the capacity to use all three of these instincts, but one of them is usually dominant, and that dominant subtype can strongly impact how your distinct Enneagram type looks to the rest of us.

The Endearing Two (Sp)

Self-Preservation Twos use a more childlike, easygoing, and innocent demeanor to have their needs met. They attract the love and attention they want by being seen as needy without having to demand anything. Typically very likable, these Twos are more aware of their physical boundaries and needs than the other Two subtypes, which is what makes them the countertype.

The Grapevine Two (So)

Social Twos don't just hear it from the grapevine; they *are* the proverbial grapevine. These Twos feel needed and loved when they are at the center of social groups and communities. Assertive, visionary, and passionate, they know how to work a room. Integrative9.com mentions that these Twos may subconsciously "give more than they are able to get back as a strategy to distract them from uncomfortable feelings," meaning these Twos' favorite mode of distraction from their own needs is to keep moving. This subtype prides themselves on being the glue of their social groups, and they are the least likely to mistype themselves compared to other Twos.

The Lover Two (Sx)

One-to-One Twos are much more focused on helping and being needed in a few intimate relationships than the other two subtypes. Yes, they love to help everyone, but they know that's not a logical goal, so they appease themselves by being the *end all/be all* to a few people. These Twos struggle with boundaries, and hearing *no* within relationships feels like a personal rejection.

So I'm a Two. What Now?

Why should I, as a type Two, embark on sixty days of devotions?

Whether you have just realized you are a type Two on the Enneagram, or have known that fact for some time, you've probably thought, *Okay, but what now? I get that I'm the Helper, that I crave love, greatly value relationships, and struggle with asking for help. The question is, how do I take this self-awareness and turn it into practical transformation?*

Some Enneagram teachers will tell you that you need only to focus on self-actualization and pull yourself up by your proverbial bootstraps to grow out of your worst behaviors. "Meditate!" they say. "Focus on yourself!" Yet, at the same time, they tell you, "Stop doing too much and rest."

However, I'm here to offer a different foundation for growth. As Christians, we know that we are flawed, sinful, and far from God's intended plan for humanity. The hymn, "Come Thou Fount of Every Blessing," includes the lyrics, "Prone to wander, Lord, I feel it." This speaks to the reality of our hearts and their rebellious nature toward our Savior.

This wandering is the problem, sin is the problem, and we are the problem! So, anyone who tells us that we ought to focus on ourselves to find growth will only lead us to more confusion. We may even find ourselves back where we started, as we go around and around this idea of focusing on self.

But we are not without hope. Philippians 1:6 says, *"I am sure of this, that he who began a good work in you will bring it to completion at the day of Jesus Christ."* On the very day you acknowledged Jesus as your Savior, repented from your sin, and dedicated your life to Him, He began a good work in your life. This work is called sanctification, which is the act of becoming holy. Your sanctification will not be finished here on earth, but you are in the process of *becoming*, day by day, moment by moment, only by the Holy Spirit's work and power within you.

We might not know how to articulate it, but this work of sanctification is the growth and change we long for. All of us know we are not who we want to be. Reflecting on the human condition in Romans 7:15, Paul said, *"For I do not understand my own actions. For I do not do what I want, but I do the very thing I hate."* Isn't that the truth?

We all know we have this haunting *potential* that always seems just a little out of reach. We all have this nagging feeling that we were created for more…but how do we get there? Only by God's grace and power within us can we rest in His sanctifying work and trust Him for the growth and potential of bringing glory to Him day by day. Only God can sanctify us, but it is our responsibility to be *"slaves of righteousness"* (Romans 6:18) and obey Him.

Over the next sixty days, we want to take you day by day through what God says about your specific problems as a Two, and how He wants to lovingly sanctify you into being more like Jesus.

The lens of the Enneagram gives us a great starting point for your specific pain points and strengths. We will use those to encourage you in the areas where God is reflected through you and in the areas where you need to lay down your instincts and let Him change you.

Some of these topics might be hard, but we hope you'll let the tension you feel in your heart open you up to change. This is where obedience comes in. We all have blind spots and areas we are more comfortable leaving in the dark, but God desires so much more for us. So ask Him to help you release your grip on those areas, bring them into the light, and experience the freedom repentance offers.

Helping, serving, always there,
Wanting to be the one to care.
When you are in need, I'm here.
Knowing, really knowing
Even before you ask.

Heart, comfort, home—
This is what I long to be,
Even when my best efforts fall short.

Losing myself so others can
Find themselves—
Isn't this what Jesus wants?
Isn't this the better way
To love and serve?

Wanting to break free
To love
Without needing much in return

Creating space, not solutions,
Listening hard, not forcing or manipulating
Beauty freely flowing, freely see
Growing to love and live
How Jesus delights in me to be.

—*Christine Rollings*

Your Guides For This Journey

You'll be hearing from two other writers and Enneagram coaches in the days ahead. The days in which no author is listed are written by me. On other days, I have asked these two Enneagram experts to help you on your path.

ALISON BRADLEY

Alison is the Enneagram Nine who has taught me the most about what it means to be a Nine. She has a deep love for the Lord and has already been serving her fellow Nines daily on Instagram at @9ish_andiknowit. She has recently become an Enneagram coach and has a great deal of knowledge about this entire typology.

CHRISTINE ROLLINGS

Christine is an Enneagram Two with a desire to help people understand themselves and have the words to express their stories to others. This led her to become an Enneagram coach, after finding the Enneagram helpful for naming her own strengths, longings, and struggles. She works particularly with people living cross-culturally, with their particular set of challenges and joys. Being a Two herself, she was thrilled to work on this devotional to encourage and challenge her fellow Twos.

10 Days of Being Helpful

How You Uniquely Reflect Christ

• • • • • • • • • • • **DAY 1**

Being Helpful Is Your Gift

And we urge you, brothers, admonish the idle, encourage the fainthearted, help the weak, be patient with them all.
(1 Thessalonians 5:14)

As you sat in church last Sunday, what did you notice around you? Did you see a tired mom, spit-up stains on her wrinkled shirt, whose eyes looked weary as she sipped from her travel mug? Or maybe you saw a young man whom you haven't seen before. He looked a little lost and his gaze was firmly affixed on his folded hands. You may have glanced over at Becky, who you know is recovering from surgery; she looked well, but you noticed her shifting now and then in discomfort.

Why do I know this was likely what you were doing? Because the eyes of a Helper can't help but notice needs, and dear Two, *you* are the Helper of the Enneagram. The gift of discerning needs is one that you're proficient at, and you probably started to realize this when you were very young. People don't need to tell you what they need, and they never need to ask you twice for a helping hand. You just know. You just act. This is a gift.

You have probably noticed that others don't quite see needs as you do, and maybe this has felt frustrating, but don't let it be so. This oversight in others should only highlight the gifting you hold. Not everyone sees as you do, and you're so needed.

Even in the loneliness and quiet of your work behind the scenes—hours cutting paper in the shape of onesies for a baby shower, days of fixing a bike for a kid in your neighborhood, cooking in the kitchen while everyone else is chatting—you are appreciated.

You see, Twos are glue. You're the glue that keeps families coming together around a table; you're the glue that mends hearts and fixes wrongs; you're the glue that keeps us all together. Without you, we'd all fall apart, and I have a feeling that, deep down, you know just how true that is.

SHIFT IN FOCUS

Take a moment to pray and thank God for the gift and honor of being a Helper. Borrow my words if they reflect your heart:

> Dear heavenly Father, I know at times I feel so weighed down by this gifting of being a Helper, but I know You knew exactly what You were doing when you gave this gift to me. I thank You for it. I thank You that I get to work alongside You as I care for Your children. I pray that You would help me to feel the depth of honor and appreciation for this role and that I will give the glory to You in return. Amen.

• • • • • • • • • • • • **DAY 2**

Being Helpful Is How You Show Jesus to Others

I lift up my eyes to the hills. From where does my help come? My help comes from the LORD, who made heaven and earth.
(Psalm 121:1–2)

Dearest Two, do you know you reflect God? In Genesis, God says that He made us in His image. Now, this doesn't mean we have a body like His, but rather we reflect parts of God's character to the rest of the world. It's not a perfect reflection—in fact, it's rippled and marred. However, a familiarity, a family resemblance, is still plainly evident between God and His creation.

God is so mighty, majestic, and perfect that none of us can reflect every part of Him, so we see His attributes scattered throughout the entire population. Each of us reflects Him in unique and very important ways.

From you, we see a depth of compassion like the compassion we saw from Jesus during His life on earth, and even now as He intercedes for us in heaven. We see a boldness that says, *"Here I am! Send me"* (Isaiah 6:8). We see the love that reflects the love of God. We also see helpfulness that reflects God and images the Holy Spirit as our Helper.

You show the world the very existence of Christ by reflecting these parts of His nature.

For his invisible attributes, namely, his eternal power and divine nature, have been clearly perceived, ever since the

creation of the world, in the things that have been made. So
they are without excuse. (Romans 1:20)

Often when we read that verse, we think of sunsets or the vastness of the ocean, which proclaim the glory of God. However, there is also the creation that God made in His very image—you and me. We proclaim the glory of God by reflecting the very nature of God. This is how He designed us, and it's a great honor we get to bear as His children.

In Twos, a big part of this reflection of God is helpfulness. Others can feel God tangibly help them through your actions and words. I can't tell you how often someone's kindness to me deeply and profoundly helps me to feel the kindness of God in my heart. It's a beautiful and sacred thing.

SHIFT IN FOCUS

I find that it's easy to focus on the ways we *don't* reflect God; our sin is often so loud and shameful, it demands center stage in our thoughts about ourselves. But have you ever thought about how dwelling on ways in which you *do* reflect God brings glory to Him?

As a child who smiles and says, "I got my blue eyes from my daddy" delights his father, so God is proud and delighted about the ways we reflect Him. Thinking about these things and thanking Him for them are important for having the right attitude toward ourselves as humans. We are humble, small, and wicked…yet created, adopted, and loved beyond measure.

Spend a few moments thinking about the family resemblance you have with God, and thank Him for the ways you get to reflect His nature to others.

DAY 3 • • • • • • • • • • •

Helpful Like God, Jesus, and the Holy Spirit
By Christine Rollings

Then God said, "Let us make man in our image, after our likeness."
(Genesis 1:26)

What were some of those family resemblances you noticed yesterday when you reflected on how you look like God? You may have thought more about how your helpfulness shows His character, and maybe you thought of other attributes too! You are His beloved child, dear Two, whom He delights to invite to be His hands and feet to a hurting world.

As you show His helpfulness to the world, His heart is also evident to the world through each aspect of His Trinity: God the Father, God the Son, and God the Holy Spirit. In Genesis 1:26, God said He made us in *"our"* image, meaning not just God the Father, but the entire Trinity. Today we will look at each of the members of the Holy Trinity and how God reveals His helpfulness through them.

God the Father is present and near to us, available to hear our cry and to help us. He gives us what we need when we ask, and He delights in giving good gifts! (See Matthew 7:9–11.) Even so, because God is all-knowing, He knows what we need even before we ask! (See Psalm 139:4.) God is the Father of mercies and comfort, and His helpfulness is seen in how He comforts us in our pain. (See 2 Corinthians 1:3–4.)

God the Father also shows us that it is good and loving to say *no*. How many times in your life have you asked God for something and heard "No" or "Wait"? He wants good things for us, even if it's not what we want at the time. He shows us that being helpful may not be received with gratitude.

God the Son, Jesus Christ, knows our physical limitations and our pain. He is Emmanuel, God dwelling among us. In His time on earth, we see His helpfulness tangibly through His ministry, through His teaching, healing, and performing of miracles. He is God who came to fulfill the law, to cure leprosy, and to feed five thousand.

He shows us that being helpful also means taking time away to care for ourselves. (See Matthew 14:23.) He also shows us that being helpful isn't easy. He came to give His life as a ransom for many (see Matthew 20:28), and right before He died, He asked the Father for another way that wouldn't include such a death (see Luke 22:42).

Jesus called God the Holy Spirit *"another Helper"* (John 14:26). Sent by God the Father, the Holy Spirit teaches us and reminds us what Jesus taught and did. He is present with us, and by His power, we have hope. (See Romans 15:13.) God the Holy Spirit also shows us that being helpful often requires us to tell the truth, even if it's hard to speak or to hear. He also gives us the boldness to speak. (See 2 Timothy 1:7.)

SHIFT IN FOCUS

Did some of those descriptions of God's helpfulness surprise you? Did you resonate with one or more of them, seeing His character on display in your own life?

Choose one or two passages of Scripture I listed above and read them. Reflect on how you have needed God's help in your life. How have you seen Him respond as God the Father, God the Son, and God the Holy Spirit?

● ● ● ● ● ● ● ● ● ● ● **DAY 4**

Martha: Serving Is Not the Problem
By Christine Rollings

Now as they went on their way, Jesus entered a village. And a woman named Martha welcomed him into her house. And she had a sister called Mary, who sat at the Lord's feet and listened to his teaching. But Martha was distracted with much serving. And she went up to him and said, "Lord, do you not care that my sister has left me to serve alone? Tell her then to help me." But the Lord answered her, "Martha, Martha, you are anxious and troubled about many things, but one thing is necessary. Mary has chosen the good portion, which will not be taken away from her."
(Luke 10:38–42)

If you're anything like me, you've heard a sermon or two about the story of Mary and Martha. It usually ends with something like this: "Are you a Mary or a Martha?" or "We need to be more like Mary." We read the story, and we hear that Mary did the better thing because she sat before the Lord, while Martha was reprimanded because of her serving.

Dear Helper, I know this can feel discouraging. Over the past few days, we have discussed how your helpfulness reflects the very heart of God. There is no shame in serving. Let me say that again, so you can let it sink deep into your heart: there is no shame in serving. Jesus Himself came to serve. (See Matthew 20:28.)

In fact, Martha's service was very important! In this passage, she had just welcomed Jesus and His disciples into her house. (See Luke 10:38.) I imagine this kicked her hospitality into full gear: running to the market, preparing a meal, making sure everyone had enough to drink.

Serving wasn't the problem. People needed to eat; the disciples needed a place to stay. And Martha was more than willing to meet that need; in fact, I imagine she was *glad* to meet that need. Her problem was that she was distracted by serving.

Currently, I'm preparing to go on a trip to visit family. Flying with an infant for the first time has me feeling anxious, and I am making lists for my lists to manage the stress. I still need to get those last-minute items and pack, and we need to get to the airport on time. But as I let my preparations take over, I miss out on the excitement of the trip, and I miss out on quality time with my husband and daughter.

The lesson of the story isn't that Martha shouldn't have served. The point isn't that serving is less important than sitting at Jesus's feet. The point of the story, what Jesus reprimanded Martha for, is that the serving distracted her from His presence.

SHIFT IN FOCUS

Have you felt shame as you read this passage of Scripture? Have you felt as if your gift of serving was bad? Dear Helper, you are a gift to those around you. Read through the passage above one more time. See the kindness of Jesus in His words. Hear His words as an invitation, rather than condemnation.

• • • • • • • • • • • **DAY 5**

Martha: A Heart Focused on Jesus
By Christine Rollings

But one thing is necessary. Mary has chosen the good portion,
which will not be taken away from her.
(Luke 10:42)

When I am in the throes of helping—the kind that gets my hands dirty and my heart pumping, the kind that makes me move quickly and fills my calendar—I tell myself that I'm doing this to serve Jesus and to serve others. It exhausts me, and it gives me a high; I feed off the adrenaline and the gratitude. I say yes to one more thing. I feel proud that I can help one more person.

I imagine Martha could have felt this way too. There are different theories as to the context and exact events of this passage, but the lessons still hold true. Martha was serving and helping— maybe she was welcoming a large group of Jesus's disciples into her home to spend a night or two. She was preparing beds and cooking food. And maybe she got a rush from all of the activity. Maybe it made her feel good and proud to be serving and preparing for her beloved Teacher and His friends.

And maybe she was exhausted.

She did, after all, ask Jesus to entreat Mary to help her. She wanted another set of hands. She had too much on her plate, and things were starting to fall off.

Maybe she told herself that she was doing this to serve Jesus. Perhaps she considered this to be an act of worship.

Maybe you've said the same thing, that you can't say *no* to things, that you're needed—your people need you; Jesus needs you. Maybe you're convinced that this is how you worship best, through taking action and helping. While it is a joy to serve Jesus, God wants us to serve *with* Jesus.

When we focus our hearts on Jesus, we partner with Him as we serve. In this, we are reminded that we don't serve for ourselves—it's not for an adrenaline rush or for gratitude. We get to be the hands and feet of Jesus to those around us. We get to sit at His feet and serve with Him.

Mary chose the good portion. It is good to sit with Jesus; it is necessary to focus our hearts on Him. It is a joy to serve with a heart that is partnered with Christ and does not run off ahead.

SHIFT IN FOCUS

In what ways are you serving today? Write down one or two here. Maybe your service is caring for a friend or a child, feeding people, or sending a word of encouragement to a friend.

1. _____

2. _____

Think about what it would look like to do these things alongside Jesus and not just for Jesus. Would it change what you're doing? Would it change the way you look at it? Invite Him into your service as you sit at His feet and serve your people.

DAY 6 • • • • • • • • • • • •

Martha: The Danger of Comparison
By Christine Rollings

But Martha was distracted with much serving. And she went up to him and said, "Lord, do you not care that my sister has left me to serve alone? Tell her then to help me."
(Luke 10:40)

My family used to gather around the television every Sunday night to watch the show *Touched by an Angel*. There was a common plot point woven throughout the drama: the angel, Monica, always wanted the gift of singing. Her friend Tess had a beautiful voice, and Monica longed to glorify God with a gift like that. But it wasn't hers to offer. (I remember cringing when she tried to sing "Danny Boy" in one of the episodes.) Instead, Monica offered the Lord and the people she watched over the gift of understanding, empathy, and kindness.

As a child watching this, I thought, *Clearly singing isn't her gift. When will she understand that?*

Now I understand a bit better.

I'm constantly comparing my calling. I look at the women who make meals every time people need it, and I long to have the capacity and the cooking skills to serve in that way. And truth be told, I wish I could sing better too.

There are also days when there are lots of diapers to change and a bathroom to clean, and I ask, *Lord, do you not care that my husband is off at work having meetings over coffee?*

It's assumed that Martha sometimes sat by Jesus's feet and listened to His teaching, as the Gospels mention her as His follower. And we know that Jesus loved her very much. (See John 11:5.) It's clear that Martha felt a closeness with Jesus; there is a familiarity in her words.

Jesus's answer here reminds me of His response to Peter when he was wondering who would betray the Lord and asked Him, *"What about this man [John]?"* (John 21:21). Jesus's replies to both Peter and Martha sound like this: *Stay in your own lane. Don't worry about what this person is doing.* Jesus said to Peter, *"You follow me!"* (John 21:22); He told Martha that she was anxious and that what Mary had chosen was good.

Your calling looks different than mine. Your calling looks different than the calling of your brother or your sister, your friend, or your spouse. Jesus invites us to focus only on what He has called us to do, how He has invited us to serve and to be.

SHIFT IN FOCUS

While you serve and help others, do you find yourself comparing your calling to those around you? You may feel jealous of another person's calling, like Monica felt about Tess in *Touched by an Angel*. You may question your brother's calling, like Peter did to John. Or you may compare callings with a heart of self-importance like I do with my husband and like Martha did with Mary.

As you consider your comparison, what do you imagine Jesus saying to you?

● ● ● ● ● ● ● ● ● ● ● ● **DAY 7**

When Helping Gets Distorted
By Christine Rollings

I am the vine; you are the branches. Whoever abides in me
and I in him, he it is that bears much fruit,
for apart from me you can do nothing.
(John 15:5)

One of the more common names for an Enneagram Two is *the Helper*. When you discovered that Two was your number, did you resonate with that title right away? Did you picture those long days serving at church or in your community? Did you picture preparing meals, running errands, and texting a sick friend, "I'm running to the store; what can I pick up for you?"

Although Twos can see this gift woven throughout their lives, helping often looks different in each season. In some seasons, the title *Helper* may become more consuming. This may look like weeks on call with a hurting friend, care coordination for a sick person at church, or the early months of motherhood with a dependent newborn.

The danger for those of us who are Helpers is confusing our desire to be needed with our worthiness of love.

We may think that we are unloved if our hurting friend doesn't call us, our sick friend no longer needs our help, or our child becomes more self-sufficient.

Our worth and our identity are not dependent on our service to others.

John 15:5 reminds us that apart from Jesus, we can do nothing. Our helpfulness is a gift, not an identity. Helping gets distorted when we use it to get the love we crave, or when we run ahead and can't sit and be with Jesus. We find ourselves only as valuable as what we can give. But our gift isn't ours to begin with. Our helping is the work of Jesus Himself and comes from an abundance of love overflowing in our lives for those around us. Our identity is in *Him*, not in our work.

SHIFT IN FOCUS

Are there certain helping tasks that define you more than others? Here are some examples:

Parent

Spouse

Leader

Counselor

Best friend

While these all are good and necessary roles, they can easily be confused with our identity. Dear Two, your true identity is a beloved child of God. Consider what your helping roles are right now. Would you feel less worthy or loved without them?

● ● ● ● ● ● ● ● ● ● ● ● **DAY 8**

When Being Helpful Is a Burden
By Christine Rollings

But he [Jesus] said to me, "My grace is sufficient for you,
for my power is made perfect in weakness."
Therefore I will boast all the more gladly of my weaknesses,
so that the power of Christ may rest upon me.
(2 Corinthians 12:9)

A good friend once shared with me that in different seasons, we have different sized plates of capacity. In some seasons, we may have the capacity of a serving platter, helping others, being on call for friends, and taking care of ourselves all at the same time. In another season, we may have a teacup or a tiny doll plate, able to carry out only necessary tasks. And sometimes, we may be somewhere in between.

When our plate is small, our constant drive to help other people may actually be a burden to us. We may want to help those around us and meet the needs we see, but it takes more energy than we have to offer—mentally, emotionally, and even physically. Now, sometimes this means that in these tiny-plate seasons, the helping is not ours to do. And sometimes we may still help, even though the cost is greater.

It's all about counting the costs of your serving, and realizing that your tiny plate will be this way only for a season. Stepping away from a responsibility or saying no may actually open up doors for others to realize their gift of serving, and there will always be more service opportunities when seasons change.

Being helpful is a gift, dear Two, but it can also be a burden. The weight of helping may be heavier than you can carry in particular seasons. You may feel overwhelmed, overcommitted, and on the road to burnout. This is not a bad thing; this simply reveals your limited capacity. That's the weakness that can show off God's power! That might mean God giving you the strength to help when you feel like you can't do it, or it might mean you releasing the need to help and trusting God with that situation.

SHIFT IN FOCUS

Do you feel like your helpfulness can be a burden? When you feel the heaviness of helping, ask yourself these questions:

Is this service my responsibility?

How can I ask others for help?

Where is God's power made perfect in my weakness? (See 2 Corinthians 12:9.)

• • • • • • • • • • • DAY 9

When Helping Is Not Yours to Do
By Christine Rollings

Each one must give as he has decided in his heart, not reluctantly or under compulsion, for God loves a cheerful giver.
(2 Corinthians 9:7)

Helping isn't always yours to do.

Do you know, dear Two, that while Jesus walked on this earth, He did not consider all of the helping His to do? He spent time in the desert before His ministry; He went away to pray. And if Jesus stepped away from the crowds, so should we.

There are so many needs and hurts that I see. Sometimes it just takes a scroll on social media or a look around my neighborhood or church sanctuary on a Sunday morning. Sometimes I even get fired up by crowdfunding websites, wishing that I could help fund them all!

But the truth is this: I have limited resources. I have limited time, money, and energy, and I cannot help every time I see a need.

Sometimes, helping is not mine to do.

Sometimes helping isn't yours to do either.

My friend Madeline, who is also a Two, recently told me this story:

> Early in my volunteering days, there was always this big annual event. There were only two employees, one

was the founder, the other was the director herself, and there would be so much pressure for the volunteers to overwork. I was working twelve hours a day, which is way too much for a volunteer. Before knowing about the Enneagram, when this would happen, I'd fall into the trap and feel like it would be wrong for me to set a boundary and not do every single thing that was asked.

Now I set boundaries before we begin and say I can volunteer only so many hours and perform only so many tasks, and I don't force myself to go in when I'm super sick. Now I actually enjoy the serving more because I'm in control and don't feel taken advantage of, instead of being exhausted and miserable once I hit my limit!

As a Christian Two, we can get so easily trapped in "if it's helping a good cause, or creating a good thing, then I must do it." But that is not true, and it's not what Jesus wants for us; He always says to pray and ask Him first and to use wisdom. There is a time for everything, different seasons and different callings.

Madeline made such a good observation. Maybe today isn't the season for helping. Perhaps it's too much in the season you are in. Perhaps you don't have the resources to help in a particular way right now. Sometimes helping is not yours to do; it may not be the best thing for that person or situation.

Helping also isn't yours to do if you're being forced into it. That isn't helping. Paul encourages the Corinthians to not give under compulsion and to not give reluctantly (see 2 Corinthians

9:7); helping isn't always yours to do when you don't want to do it. Our helping is a delight to God when we do it cheerfully!

SHIFT IN FOCUS

Let this be the permission you need to hear that you don't need to always be the one to help.

All helping, whether enjoyed or not, should be a decision between you and the Lord. If you feel the pull on your heart that what you're doing right now might not *all* be yours to do, then bring it to Him. He'll give you the wisdom to sort it out. (See James 1:5.)

DAY 10 • • • • • • • • • • • •

How Do I Know What's Mine to Help With?
By Alison Bradley

For each will have to bear his own load.
(Galatians 6:5)

When helping is your strength, the lines of what belongs to you and what belongs to someone else can easily become blurred. You see so clearly what needs to be done, and it may be challenging to not do more than is yours. How do you know what is yours alone?

Let's look at Galatians 6. Pay attention to areas of resonance and resistance within your heart as you read.

> *Bear one another's burdens, and so fulfill the law of Christ. For if anyone thinks he is something, when he is nothing, he deceives himself. But let each one test his own work, and then his reason to boast will be in himself alone and not in his neighbor. For each will have to bear his own load.*
>
> (Galatians 6:2–5)

In this passage, Paul talks about both bearing one another's burdens and bearing your own load. This isn't a contradiction. There are times when you partner with the Lord to care for someone. There are also times when you have to let others do their own load-bearing. Paul explains how to discern the difference: *"Let each one test his own work."*

What is your motivation for helping? It may be hard to sort out initially, but as with any skill, you'll get better the more you practice checking in with your own heart and the Lord about why you're helping. If you're not sure, then pause and ask the Lord to help you discern why you want to help.

Galatians 6:5 offers a gentle and sobering reminder for our hearts: *"For each will have to bear his own load."* Each of us answers to the Lord and the Lord alone for his or her actions. You are not responsible for anyone but yourself. Just as you will answer for all your actions to the Lord, so will everyone else. You will answer for your motivations for helping; did you help out of humility or in hopes of looking good or getting something later on?

You will answer for the times your intervention was unhelpful, taking on others' responsibilities instead of allowing them to reap the consequences of their actions. It can be painful to allow someone to carry the weight of their choices, but it is more unloving to remove those consequences for them.

Paul continues, *"Do not be deceived: God is not mocked, for whatever one sows, that will he also reap"* (Galatians 6:7). The Lord can help you discern the most loving response in any given circumstance. May this be a freeing reminder of truth for your heart: You are responsible only for you.

SHIFT IN FOCUS

As you practice discerning what is yours, these questions might be helpful. Answer them as honestly as you can, and ask the Holy Spirit to reveal the true state of your heart.

Why do I want to help this person?

How will I feel if they say no to my offer of help?

How will I feel if I don't receive any reciprocation for helping?

Is this truly a loving response or is this for my own comfort?

Is the Lord asking this of me?

10 Days of Killing Pride
How the Enemy Wants to Stop You from Reflecting God

• • • • • • • • • • • DAY 11

What Is a Deadly Sin?

If anyone is caught in any transgression, you who are spiritual should restore him in a spirit of gentleness. Keep watch on yourself, lest you too be tempted.
(Galatians 6:1)

Although the Bible does not mention the *seven deadly sins,* Christians have known about them for ages. The classification of these sins was first penned by Evagrius Ponticus, a monk who lived from 345–399 AD. This list has gone through many changes over the years, but it has remained a helpful way for us to name the vices that keep us in chains.

Each of these seven sins can be paired with an Enneagram number (with two extra sins to total nine) to give us a better idea of the specific vice that may be tripping up each type. This is important information because these vices are often blind spots to us, and their exposure leads to repentance and greater unity with Christ, which is the greatest thing learning about our Enneagram number can do for us.

Here are the deadly sins early Enneagram teachers paired with each type:

1. Anger
2. Pride
3. Deceit
4. Envy
5. Greed

6. Fear
7. Gluttony
8. Lust
9. Sloth

This idea of struggling with one dominant sin does not mean that you do not struggle with any or all of these sins. We can all recognize ourselves in each of those sins. However, the dominant deadly sin paired with your Enneagram type is a specific tool that Satan will use to distract you from seeing how you reflect God.

For Twos, the deadly sin is pride, and whether or not you recognize pride in your own life, I encourage you to give it great thought as you read these coming chapters.

Exposing blind spots in our lives can feel a lot like ripping off a bandage that we might prefer to leave on, but what's underneath is God-honoring and beautiful.

SHIFT IN FOCUS

Spend some time contemplating and praying about what pride might look like in your life.

Does it surprise you to see that sin printed next to your Enneagram number?

• • • • • • • • • • • • **DAY 12**

What Is Pride?

The pride of your heart has deceived you, you who live in the
clefts of the rock, in your lofty dwelling, who say in your heart,
"Who will bring me down to the ground?"
(Obadiah 1:3)

Pride can be a difficult topic; while we don't want to be seen as prideful, it's a sin that is not given as much weight as others. One way we diminish the sin of pride is by saying things like "Well, everyone is prideful!"

Pride shows up in the lives of Twos when they believe that they alone know how to help people. They may complain about being too busy, but they're very unlikely to delegate their load.

Pride says, "They're too busy and they wouldn't do this job as well as I do." "See, I'm helping everyone by just doing it myself." "I guess I'll have to do this, or it won't get done." "They'll praise me when they see what a good job I did with this!"

Pride assumes many things, one of which is others' unwillingness and your own superiority for doing what others are unwilling to do. Stepping up and completing a thankless task is not always bad, but what's going on in your heart? Do you assume others won't help?

Pride often disguises itself in the lives of Twos by putting on the masks of control, high standards, strong work ethics, and service to those around you.

SHIFT IN FOCUS

Spend some time asking God to reveal any pride that has been hiding in your life.

● ● ● ● ● ● ● ● ● ● ● ● **DAY 13**

How Satan Wants to Stop You from Reflecting God

Be sober-minded; be watchful. Your adversary the devil prowls
around like a roaring lion, seeking someone to devour.
(1 Peter 5:8)

Earlier in this devotional, we talked about how you reflect God (see days 1 and 2) and what that means for you as a Two. But with that honor comes a cost. We have an enemy because our God has an enemy. This enemy, Satan, does not want God's image to reflect clearly through us, and so he seeks to destroy us. If Satan can't have our eternity, he will endeavor to steal our testimony, our peace, and our joy.

Satan does not want God's love, helpfulness, and empathy clearly shown to others through Twos. Every loving thought, every kind idea, and every hand raised are enough to make Satan want to throw a chair out the window. He can't stand it.

So what does he do? He's sneaky, and he's smart, so he tells Twos, "That was your idea." "See, you're so kind." "You just have such a beautiful heart." "These people are lucky to have you." "Only you can fulfill this role, and you never get the appreciation you deserve." These feel-good thoughts are sweeter than honey and they're making us fat with pride.

If Satan can't get you to stop, he will tempt you to steal the glory of your actions from God. Pride means that instead of humbly returning the glory of your service to the Creator who made you, and whose image you reflect, you soak it up for yourself. This is pride, and it works to stop you imaging God to others.

SHIFT IN FOCUS

I know this may be a really hard pill to swallow, but I desperately want you to be aware of this sin and call it what it is. No, this might not be all of you, but don't let what isn't true about this distract you from what might be.

Yes, we all struggle with pride, but that doesn't give us a free pass not to fight it.

I encourage you to reflect on what has been said and watch your heart as you serve. What might you need to let others take over or help you with? What do you enjoy doing? Maybe God is asking you to do more of what you really enjoy and to delegate some of your other tasks.

• • • • • • • • • • • DAY 14

How Satan Uses Pride to Stop You

So, whether you eat or drink, or whatever you do,
do it to the glory of God.
(1 Corinthians 10:31)

Satan uses pride to hide how Twos reflect God. When we let pride make itself at home in our hearts, then we start to soak up all the glory that belongs to God. Prideful hearts will also shift our focus on the feedback we're receiving and how well or poorly others are reciprocating our kindness instead of why we're doing it in the first place. You see, discontentment and selfishness are the best friends of pride. We'll rarely find one without the others.

If Satan can win in this area, then others will start to reject our offers of help. The price is too high when they can't repay us or might even forget to thank us. A prideful heart says, "I will do this so that you will honor and glorify me!" A prideful heart keeps a record of every good thing it's done as proof that it should be treated better and is worthy of love. Keeping record of our giving is not generosity. Giving with an expectation of getting something in return (without explicitly saying so) is manipulative.

Most people can sense a prideful heart before they can name it. If this is the case, they won't want your help, charity, generosity, or gifts. This is how Satan stops you from reflecting helpfulness and generosity in Christ's love: he inflates the price for your help, and that's when people start to reject it.

Of course, there are other reasons people refuse your help that have nothing to do with your pride, but when pride is on full display, the no's start rolling in. They may even end with the ultimate no—a no to friendship or a relationship of any kind.

In contrast, a humble heart says, *"Here I am"* (Isaiah 6:8); I will serve even if I receive nothing in return. A humble heart is not focused on its reward here on earth because it knows its reward is in heaven. It doesn't need your applause or thanks to feel fulfilled.

I think all of us need to grow in this area of humility. Amen?

When Twos grow in humility, they become greater beacons of God's love, generosity, and helpfulness. If you're trying to proclaim these things in your own strength, it's going to cost your mental health and relationships and particularly hinder your relationship with God. But when you humbly offer to God all the praise and glory you receive, then you are no longer in competition for it. You can have peace, rest, and an unhindered relationship with the God who loves you.

SHIFT IN FOCUS

What would it look like to shift your focus to your reward in heaven?

Consider memorizing Matthew 6:19–21:

> Do not lay up for yourselves treasures on earth, where moth and rust destroy and where thieves break in and steal, but lay up for yourselves treasures in heaven, where neither moth nor rust destroys and where thieves do not break in and steal. For where your treasure is, there your heart will be also.

● ● ● ● ● ● ● ● ● ● ● ● **DAY 15**

The Sneaky Voice of Pride
By Christine Rollings

> *The thief comes only to steal and kill and destroy.*
> *I came that they may have life and have it abundantly.*
> (John 10:10)

Do you hear that sneaky voice of pride in your heart? Do you know what it sounds like?

Most of the time, I don't even know it's there. Pride has a way of whispering in my heart in a way that makes me feel safe and comfortable. It's a scroll through social media after a long day, looking at photos of smiling faces and accomplishments, and telling myself, "I'm doing better than they are." And before I can stop it, I find my worth there, in the comparison.

Pride sounds like the unwillingness to admit that I was wrong, especially when I'd thought my intentions were good. I find my worth there, in my own understanding.

Pride sounds like my impatience while waiting in traffic or in line at the store, thinking that my time is worth more than others'. I find my worth there, in my self-importance.

What does pride sound like for you?

Pride tells us that we are more important than others. Pride tells us that we can do it on our own. Pride can even tell us, ever so subtly, that we don't need Jesus.

Jesus came so we wouldn't have to rely on our own self-importance for our worth. He came so we wouldn't need to compare ourselves to others to feel good enough. He came so that we would have life abundantly. He came to defeat sin, death, and pride so that we would feel safe and valued in Him. He came so that we would live out of the fullness of His love for us—a love that we cannot earn or lose, that has no end or height or depth. God wants us to live with the assurance that we are loved like that.

SHIFT IN FOCUS

Consider what pride sounds like to you. Did one of these examples resonate with you? Underline or circle the text. Did these examples bring to mind another one? Write it down here.

_____

_____

As God sheds light on your pride in the coming weeks, months, and years, what might it look like for you to choose humility instead of pride?

• • • • • • • • • • • DAY 16

How to Spot a Prideful Thought
By Christine Rollings

God shows his love for us in that while we were still sinners,
Christ died for us.
(Romans 5:8)

Dear Two, we love comfort, and we love to be loved. This is the epitome of our number—the desire to be loved and wanted. This is a good desire! At its core, it points us to Jesus; He wants us and loves us unconditionally, showing His love for us *"while we were still sinners."* It's when we build our life around the love we receive from the world that we stop reflecting Christ.

I'm comfortable with the picture I have of myself: this person knows what she's doing and is kind to other people. She is loving and always willing to help someone in need. But when someone confronts me with a different version of myself, I get defensive. That's when I see my pride most clearly. I am so intent on maintaining this picture of myself that I'm unwilling to humbly look at how I've poorly reflected Christ. How prideful is it to assume I don't have any flaws or concerns and to fight anyone who might try to tell me that I do?

These prideful thoughts are hard to spot; they're not always as obvious as other sins. Pride feels comforting, like a warm blanket we can hide under on a rainy day. But that's how we can tell a prideful thought is there: when we try to take off the blanket, is it hard to remove? Is it easier to stay under it?

We work so hard to keep this idea of ourselves that we stop reflecting Christ. He is shown to the world through our weaknesses, which can't be seen when we are working so hard to cover them up.

> *But he said to me, "My grace is sufficient for you, for my power is made perfect in weakness." Therefore I will boast all the more gladly of my weaknesses, so that the power of Christ may rest upon me.* (2 Corinthians 12:9)

SHIFT IN FOCUS

Consider your prideful thoughts. Take a moment and pray something like this:

Dear heavenly Father, You love me even when I curl up in my safe, warm blanket of pride. You love me when I cling to a picture of myself that isn't true. In the next few days, help me to see what pride looks like in my heart. Show me how it impacts You and the people around me. Amen.

As you go through your day, pay attention to your need for that blanket of pride. Write down how you feel about this blanket now that you're aware of it.

• • • • • • • • • • • • DAY 17

Pride Versus Humility
By Christine Rollings

For by the grace given to me I say to everyone among you not to
think of himself more highly than he ought to think,
but to think with sober judgment, each according
to the measure of faith that God has assigned.
(Romans 12:3)

When we spot a prideful thought, when we see it for what it really is and how it impacts our hearts, God's heart, and those around us, what do we do? How do we train our minds, taking *"every thought captive to obey Christ"* (2 Corinthians 10:5)?

Hubris is excessive pride that makes us feel that we can do something just as well, if not better, than anyone else. In some ways, it's our attempt to protect ourselves by saying that we are competent, that we know, even better than God, what is best and what is helpful.

The opposite of this is humility. Humility is having a modest or low view of our importance. So instead of the belief that we can do it without God, it's the understanding that we need God. Instead of this false picture of myself that has it all together and can do all things, it's the recognition of Jesus's importance over my own.

Pride says, "I can do all these things because my people need me. I need to serve those around me in order to be useful."

Humility says, "I will help others, as I am able, not because I need to, but because it is a joy to serve Jesus."

This kind of humility doesn't say, "Woe is me. Who can love me?" This kind of humility is rooted in our deep knowledge of who we are in Jesus and because of Jesus. We know we are loved and valued because of who we are in Him, not because of what we do.

This kind of humility allows us to face who we truly are—flaws, weaknesses, and all—because it recognizes that God's work in us is most important.

Pride says, "I need the comfort of this high view of myself. I rely on the knowledge that I am good."

Humility says, "I know that I am weak and flawed. I rely on the knowledge of God's goodness and the sacrifice of Jesus."

"Let the one who boasts, boast in the Lord.' For it is not the one who commends himself who is approved, but the one whom the Lord commends. (2 Corinthians 10:17–18)

SHIFT IN FOCUS

The Bible has a lot to say about pride and humility. As you reflect on this, look up the following verses, and ask God to help you see your heart clearly:

+ Proverbs 11:12
+ Isaiah 2:11
+ Luke 14:11

+ 1 Corinthians 1:31

+ James 4:6

What do you learn about God's heart from these verses? What do you learn about yourself?

DAY 18 • • • • • • • • • • •

Growing in Humility
By Christine Rollings

But he said to me, "My grace is sufficient for you, for my power is made perfect in weakness." Therefore I will boast all the more gladly of my weaknesses, so that the power of Christ may rest upon me.
(2 Corinthians 12:9)

How do we grow in this view of ourselves that understands our weaknesses and dwells in Jesus's goodness?

I find myself fighting between two extremes. One extreme comes from a place of pride: I feel like I can and I want to do things myself and for myself, safely inside my cocoon of self-delusion. Pride says, "I'm a good person who rarely makes mistakes and who finds value in helping others." The other extreme is self-pity, which is also self-centered and self-serving, and which comes from a heart of pride. Self-pity says, "I'm not a good person, I always mess up, and I don't know how to help others."

These places are neither holy nor true. They do not come from dwelling in the truth of who God is and who I am in light of that. Recognizing this is where a heart of humility comes.

Growing in humility is a daily practice. It does not come easily, and we do not finish it on this side of eternity. I think that this growth looks a lot like *abiding*.

I am the true vine, and my Father is the vinedresser. Every branch in me that does not bear fruit he takes away, and every branch that does bear fruit he prunes, that it may bear more fruit. Already you are clean because of the word that I have spoken to you. Abide in me, and I in you. As the branch cannot bear fruit by itself, unless it abides in the vine, neither can you, unless you abide in me. I am the vine; you are the branches. Whoever abides in me and I in him, he it is that bears much fruit, for apart from me you can do nothing. If anyone does not abide in me he is thrown away like a branch and withers; and the branches are gathered, thrown into the fire, and burned. If you abide in me, and my words abide in you, ask whatever you wish, and it will be done for you. By this my Father is glorified, that you bear much fruit and so prove to be my disciples. As the Father has loved me, so have I loved you. Abide in my love. If you keep my commandments, you will abide in my love, just as I have kept my Father's commandments and abide in his love. These things I have spoken to you, that my joy may be in you, and that your joy may be full. (John 15:1–11)

When we abide in Christ, we let go of our self-importance.

When we abide in Christ, we have no room for self-sufficiency.

When we abide in Christ, we have no need for self-protection.

When we abide in Christ, we let His love sustain us and define us.

SHIFT IN FOCUS

Read through John 15:1–11 again.

What does it look like for you to abide in Jesus today?

What happens to your pride when you abide in Jesus?

How does this grow your heart in humility?

• • • • • • • • • • • **DAY 19**

A Biblical Example of Pride: Growing in Humility like Peter
By Christine Rollings

Humble yourselves, therefore, under the mighty hand of God
so that at the proper time he may exalt you, casting all
your anxieties on him, because he cares for you.
(1 Peter 5:6–7)

The Bible is filled with stories of life change. One of my favorites is the story of the apostle Peter. We get to learn so much from him as his story appears in the Gospels and Acts, and then we read his own words in his letters.

When I picture Peter, I imagine this gung-ho, all-in, shoot-for-the-moon kind of guy. He was zealous and ready for action. Immediately, he left his net to follow Jesus (see Matthew 4:20), he spoke the truth about Jesus (see Matthew 16:16), and he was commissioned by Jesus (see Matthew 16:18). He was the one to rise (and then sink) to the occasion of walking on water (see Matthew 14:22–33) and the one to vow undying loyalty to Jesus only to fall asleep in the garden as Jesus prayed (see Matthew 26:37–40).

We see Peter's pride in his sense of self-importance when he rebuked Jesus. (See Matthew 16:22.) We see his reliance on self when he told Jesus, *"Though they all fall away because of you, I will never fall away"* (Matthew 26:33). Finally, we see his pride in his self-protection when he denied knowing Jesus three times after Jesus had been arrested. (See Matthew 26:69–75.)

But Peter's story didn't end there. In the book of Acts, Peter not only preached boldly and led the disciples, but he declared before a council of religious leaders, "*We must obey God rather than man*" (Acts 5:29). Peter was growing to proclaim who he served!

"*Humble yourselves, therefore,*" he wrote in his first letter to churches in Asia Minor, "*under the mighty hand of God so that at the proper time he may exalt you, casting all your anxieties on him, because he cares for you*" (1 Peter 5:6–7).

These words came from a leader who had grown in humility. He was rebuked, questioned, and even arrested, and he stood firm in the truth of who Jesus was. Instead of seeing himself as important, he learned to boast only in Christ. Instead of relying on His strength, he relied on the strength and guidance of the Holy Spirit. Instead of protecting himself, he faced danger and opposition for the name of Jesus. In humility, Peter demonstrated his freedom in Christ.

SHIFT IN FOCUS

Where do you see yourself in Peter's growth journey from pride to humility? It isn't an either-or; when we learn to walk in humility, we may still struggle with pride. As we look over Peter's life throughout Scripture, we can see that He walked more and more in humility with God.

What about you? Are you eager and zealous like Peter was in the Gospels? Are you learning to walk in your calling as Peter did in the book of Acts? Are you sharing the wisdom of what you have learned through trials as Peter did in his letters?

DAY 20 • • • • • • • • • • • •

Defeating Pride in Your Life
By Christine Rollings

Let the one who boasts, boast in the Lord.
(1 Corinthians 1:31)

When my pride gets called out, the vulnerability I experience is piercing. My first reaction is to feel unloved and unworthy of being loved. Pride is ugly, and who can love me when they know my pride?

But that isn't what God says. God's story doesn't end with my pride. When my pride is exposed, God's grace shines the brightest. James wrote, "*But he gives more grace. Therefore [Scripture] says, 'God opposes the proud but gives grace to the humble'*" (James 4:6).

"*He gives more grace.*"

When my pride is exposed, it begins to loosen its grip on me, releasing me to desperately seek God. In that desperation, God gives more grace.

James went on to explain exactly how to defeat pride: "*Submit yourselves therefore to God*" (James 4:7).

Here is where we see ourselves in light of who God is. We are His children, dependent on Him for our every breath. And in Him, we are safe to see ourselves for who we really are. Here, we are safe and we are loved.

"Resist the devil, and he will flee from you" (James 4:7). Our pride keeps us trapped and keeps us from experiencing God's grace. The devil does not want us to experience God's grace! But with Jesus's power, the devil will flee. Jesus's power is stronger.

"Draw near to God, and he will draw near to you" (James 4:8). We can draw near to Him without fear of rejection, without fear of being unloved. *"While we were still sinners, Christ died for us"* (Romans 5:8). We are already seen, and we are already loved.

Cleanse your hands, you sinners, and purify your hearts, you double-minded. Be wretched and mourn and weep. Let your laughter be turned to mourning and your joy to gloom. (James 4:8–9)

In God's safe presence, we can admit that we are wrong. We can admit that our hearts are dirty and we need to be cleansed. Here we can mourn our pride and how it breaks God's heart. Our pride says we don't need Him, and that grieves His heart. We shouldn't minimize our sin by saying that pride is no big deal, it isn't as bad as other sins, or it is something everyone struggles with. We must let it grieve our hearts like it grieves God's.

"Humble yourselves before the Lord, and he will exalt you" (James 4:10). Now that our pride grieves our hearts, as it does God's, we can approach His throne with humble hearts, knowing our place before Him. It is here, when we are broken and reliant on Him, that He exalts us.

Our boasting should not be in ourselves or our accomplishments, our giving or our helpfulness. We should boast in the work of God in our lives, in His abundant grace.

SHIFT IN FOCUS

Read James 4:6–10 on your own. Stop at every sentence and consider the instruction James gives. Bring your pride before the Lord and allow Him to use this time to defeat the pride in your heart as you humble yourself before Him.

As much as we may wish, this isn't a once-and-done kind of prayer. Pride can be a constant struggle in our hearts and lives. How can this prayer of humility become a part of our faith rhythm?

10 Days of Boldness
Your Strength and How To Use It

• • • • • • • • • • • DAY 21
What Is Boldness?

Since we have such a hope, we are very bold.
(2 Corinthians 3:12)

Dear Two, would you call yourself bold?

When a friend is hurting, when there's a right thing to be done, when a meal is needed, when a host is required, when someone needs a hug, what do you do? You don't hesitate. That, my friend, is boldness.

You're not a weak or timid Two. Nurturing isn't a quiet task. You are bold, you take charge, and you do what needs to be done. There is a fight in you, and the Enneagram acknowledges this about your personality, which I think is perfect and so needed.

Boldness says, "Here I am; use me!" (See Isaiah 6:8.) Boldness says, "If you need me, I'm there." Boldness says, "I love Jesus more than I love my comfort." Boldness says, "I'm the right person for this job."

There's a confidence in boldness, but more importantly, there's obedience. Obedience requires action, and boldness is all about action.

Now you are most definitely not perfect in your boldness, but that doesn't mean it's not a strength. Over these next nine days, we'll dive deeper into what it means for you to be bold, and how to use this strength for God's glory.

SHIFT IN FOCUS

How does seeing boldness in this devotional about your Enneagram number make you feel?

Spend some time digesting what was said here. Then, identify four emotions that come to mind as you read it:

_____

_____

● ● ● ● ● ● ● ● ● ● ● **DAY 22**

Boldness versus Aggression

The wicked flee when no one pursues,
but the righteous are bold as a lion.
(Proverbs 28:1)

As you read through yesterday's devotional, perhaps you cringed at the thought of boldness describing you. Perhaps you would add aggression or pushiness to the same category, and those are not necessarily things you want to be called.

I empathize with this, as aggression is often a negative term when used in American culture, especially when it describes a woman. However, boldness and aggression don't have to be negative.

Here are positive examples:

Aggression

Mike is a father of four girls. When his oldest was twelve years old, he found out that her best friend was doing drugs. He told his daughter that she wasn't spending time with that friend anymore, and he proceeded to have a meeting with the girl's parents. He aggressively protected and advocated for the health of his child and her friend.

Boldness

Cheryl knew that the only way to repair her relationship with her mom was to stop ignoring the pain. Sitting down with her over coffee, she boldly poured out her heart, and although her mom was surprised and hurt by the conversation, they were able to move forward and enjoy a healthy mother-daughter relationship because of Cheryl's bold honesty.

Boldness could easily be described as bravery, truth-telling, sticking up for what is right, or courage, which all are good and God-honoring acts.

Now there is a negative side to these expressions.

Boldness can be out of place, especially when others' boundaries are not considered or respected. If you want to grow in God-honoring boldness, communication is key. Ask before you help others, text before you pop over, and don't push yourself on others. Communication can solve a world of hurt, and when it comes to boldness, that's doubly true.

Aggression is often seen as negative when it is used in situations that do not warrant it, such as when someone can't control his or her anger. These are obviously dangerous things. Gentleness is a better choice in many instances, but there is also a time and a place for aggression.

SHIFT IN FOCUS

Look up boldness in the dictionary, and write down its definition here:

_____

What's one positive instance of boldness you can recall from your life?

_____

_____

● ● ● ● ● ● ● ● ● ● ● ● **DAY 23**

God Gives Us Boldness
By Christine Rollings

Have I not commanded you? Be strong and courageous.
Do not be frightened, and do not be dismayed,
for the LORD your God is with you wherever you go.
(Joshua 1:9)

When God gives a command, He also provides the resources for us to obey. When He told Joshua to be strong and courageous, He did not require him to muster up the strength and courage within himself to obey. God knew that He alone had the supply that Joshua needed. The same is true for you and me!

In the early church, news of Jesus spread like wildfire. In Acts 4, Peter and John stood before rulers, elders, and scribes, answering their questions with boldness. This kind of boldness astonished the leaders! They could tell that Peter and John had been with Jesus. When these two disciples returned to their friends and reported what had happened, they prayed together and asked God for boldness for them to continue speaking the truth. God didn't wait long to answer this prayer—in the very next verse, they were filled with the Holy Spirit and continued to speak with boldness! (See Acts 4:31.)

Sometimes boldness looks like speaking a hard truth that someone needs to hear. Sometimes boldness looks like creating space for vulnerable conversations to happen. And sometimes boldness looks like believing that our voice is valuable, and we have something worthy of saying! Whether we are leading a nation like Joshua or speaking truth like Peter and John, God will give us the boldness we need.

SHIFT IN FOCUS

Jesus told us, *"Ask, and it will be given to you; seek, and you will find; knock, and it will be opened to you"* (Matthew 7:7). What in your life requires you to be bold? Maybe it's initiating a difficult conversation, starting something new, or even asking for help. Write that thing down here:

_____

_____

Now ask God to give you the boldness you need to obey Him in this. Watch Him provide it for you abundantly!

Boldness and Jesus
By Christine Rollings

Then children were brought to him that he might lay his hands on
them and pray. The disciples rebuked the people, but Jesus said,
"Let the little children come to me and do not hinder them,
for to such belongs the kingdom of heaven."
(Matthew 19:13–14)

Have you ever thought about Jesus as a man of boldness? It isn't the first characteristic of Him that comes to my mind. I first think of Jesus as kind, gentle, and patient. I think of Him as loving.

Then I read that passage about the children coming to Him, and I look at the Gospels a little closer. When He told His disciples to let the children come to Him, He was opening His heart and asking His disciples to do the same. He was inviting the vulnerable to be in a relationship with Him, and that is one of the boldest things a person can do.

Boldness isn't the first thing that comes to mind when I think of myself as a Two. I think of Twos as kind, gentle, and patient. I think of Twos as loving and wanting to be loved. But as I look at the life of Jesus, I see boldness in myself too.

Jesus modeled boldness to us in so many different ways:

+ He spoke truth with conviction.
+ He healed the sick and was there for the needy.

+ He put His reputation on the line to meet with people whom society shunned.
+ He led a group of people.
+ He got angry at the things that made God angry. (See Matthew 21:12–13.)
+ He asked His friends to be with Him in His time of need. (See Matthew 26:38.)
+ He laid His life down in obedience to God.

Jesus showed us that sometimes boldness comes naturally. For me, that looks like being willing to make a meal for a sick friend. I'd jump at the opportunity! Jesus also showed us that sometimes being bold costs us something. For me, that can be telling a family member that he or she hurt me or asking a friend for help.

SHIFT IN FOCUS

Look over the list of ways Jesus modeled boldness. Can you think of other examples from Scripture? As you read this list, consider how it might look in your life. In what situation do you speak truth with conviction? How are you asking for help in time of need? Even caring for a sick friend, dear Two, is not a passive act! It is brave, and it is bold!

• • • • • • • • • • • • **DAY 25**

Boldness in the Bible

Go, gather all the Jews to be found in Susa, and hold a fast on my behalf, and do not eat or drink for three days, night or day. I and my young women will also fast as you do. Then I will go to the king, though it is against the law, and if I perish, I perish.
(Esther 4:16)

The biblical story of Esther is a goose-bump-raising tale of boldness. She was faced with an impossible choice—ask her husband, the king, for deliverance of her people and possibly be killed for entering his presence unsummoned, or ultimately let all of her kin be killed, perhaps even herself if her heritage was discovered.

It really was the choice of die sooner or later. I have to think that most of our hearts would've chosen the latter, possibly dying later after having been discovered.

Now I'm sure Esther was sweating, shaking, and praying in those moments leading up to her bold act, but she did it anyway. It was the right thing to do, and God blessed her obedience.

Not many of us will ever be faced with a die-now-or-die-later kind of decision, but we still act with boldness. What does boldness look like in our lives?

Boldness looks like doing the right thing even if conflict may arise. Boldness looks like serving the needy and poor even in *that* part of town. Boldness looks like becoming a foster parent even if everyone thinks you're crazy. Boldness looks like giving even if you will receive nothing in return. Boldness looks like helping a friend even if you might catch her cold as a consequence.

Boldness looks like doing the right thing even if *such and such* occurs. That's boldness, and that's the boldness Esther had.

SHIFT IN FOCUS

Read Esther 4. How did she come to her decision to help? What were her fears and concerns?

● ● ● ● ● ● ● ● ● ● ● ● **DAY 26**

Loving Boldly: How You Reflect God

What do you think? If a man has a hundred sheep, and one of them has gone astray, does he not leave the ninety-nine on the mountains and go in search of the one that went astray?
(Matthew 18:12)

In this verse, we see Jesus clarifying what God's love really means. Yes, God loves the righteous and obedient, but He doesn't need to save them. No, He often leaves His sheep to find and save the lost.

This can feel like a slap in the face to those of us who are one of the ninety-nine sheep, but really, it's a beautiful picture of the lengths to which God will go to rescue us. He will find us, He will bring us back to His fold, and He will leave His other ninety-nine sheep to do so. Even if you are in the ninety-nine right now, some day you might be the one. Maybe you were already the one.

This kind of love is bold. It would have been much easier for Jesus to assume that His one sheep had already fallen prey to some predator, or that the searching would be a waste of time, or that it wouldn't be worth leaving the shade of His tree.

Going after a lost sheep is not the easy road. But God, being the bold God He is, would not hesitate. This is a bold love, dear Two, and you get the honor of reflecting this bold love to the rest of us.

_____

SHIFT IN FOCUS

Dear heavenly Father, I thank You that I reflect even a glimmer of Your bold love. Help me to be the kind of person who does the right thing without hesitation and give me the wisdom to know when those days come. Amen.

• • • • • • • • • • • **DAY 27**

Loving Boldly: How You Protect with Love

*But the Lord is faithful. He will establish you
and guard you against the evil one.*
(2 Thessalonians 3:3)

Your boldness is evident when you nurture and protect.

Twos may not be the most aggressive Enneagram number, but they are highly protective. Perhaps you can't recall many times you were physically protective. You may protect someone mentally, emotionally, and spiritually by helping and nurturing them. That's what nurturing is after all, isn't it? Protecting someone's emotional, mental, and spiritual needs is, in fact, protecting them physically.

Now, nurturing isn't present only in parent-child relationships. In fact, as an adult, you probably have people in your life who are nurturing you, and we all continually need this.

Nurturing is the process of caring for and encouraging the growth or development of someone or something. Nurturing in its simplest form is just care and encouragement, and those are some of the things Twos do best.

Nurturing looks like a gentle task from the outside, but it requires great boldness to carry out. The person you're nurturing may not feel like they need nurturing. They'll fight loving hands, they'll eat junk food, and they'll engage in dangerous behavior, and you will boldly bring them back in.

In the animal kingdom, a nurturing parent is the most protective of all animals. Think of a mother bear with her little cubs. When a bear is in a season of intense nurturing, she will boldly protect her babies, even if she has to take someone or something out, even to the point of death.

You are that mother bear when it comes to those you're protecting and nurturing. This type of love is bold, and it's very protective.

SHIFT IN FOCUS

Write down who is in your protective care right now and reflect on how you boldly love them.

_____

_____

• • • • • • • • • • • **DAY 28**

Loving Boldly: Speaking Up When Others Can't

> *Open your mouth, judge righteously,*
> *defend the rights of the poor and needy.*
> (Proverbs 31:9)

Twos are not timid creatures. If you've ever been told that or thought that, take a moment to destroy that idea in your mind right now. It's not true. "People-pleasing" and "compliance" may be used to describe Twos, and they may be a default for you, but by no means are Twos timid and unwilling to take a stand when the situation calls for it.

Twos are bold; *you* are bold, especially when you see the marginalized and mistreated.

Proverbs 31:9 says to "*open your mouth.*" This is a practical way you can love boldly, by speaking up for those who can't.

"*Judge righteously.*" Have you ever observed a situation at hand and thought, *Is this right? Is there some injustice here? Is there someone who needs protection, justice, and love?* This is judging righteously, using a sound mind and an even scale to judge.

"*Defend the rights of the poor and needy.*" We use this right judgment to decide when we need to speak up and defend the rights of others. This is not timidity, and I know that if the time came for you to speak up, you would. This is one example that you are, in fact, not timid. You are bold, and you love boldly when you see the poor and needy.

The Bible talks a lot about the orphans and widows (see James 1:27), groups that are still marginalized today. I believe that Twos make up the largest group of helpers for these groups.

Loving boldly is who you are as a Two, and it's how God is using you to change the world.

SHIFT IN FOCUS

What orphans and/or widows are within your reach today? I'm sure you already have a good grasp of the mistreated and marginalized around you, which takes a heavy toll on your heart.

How can you boldly speak up for them? What action can you take today to serve them? How have you already done this?

• • • • • • • • • • • • **DAY 29**

Loving Boldly: Saying No Can Be Loving
By Christine Rollings

But now even more the report about him went abroad, and great crowds gathered to hear him and to be healed of their infirmities. But he would withdraw to desolate places and pray.
(Luke 5:15–16)

Dear Two, saying no can be one of the hardest things to do. Saying no to a friend can feel like a big risk. It feels counter to your nature to say no when you desire to help.

But sometimes, the most loving thing you can do is to say no. Sometimes, it can be the most loving thing to another person. Sometimes, it can be the most loving thing to yourself.

Recently, I asked a friend for help with a project. The next day, she responded with a kind, "No, but thank you for thinking of me." I read her response and felt so loved! My reaction surprised me; why did I feel loved? Because she honored my request by expressing gratitude that she had been thought of, and she answered honestly. Even though it's not what I wanted, it strengthened my trust in her, knowing that she would be honest about her capacity to help in the future.

Jesus came to earth with a clear vision of what was His to do. Throughout the Gospels, He clarified His vision to His disciples: He came to heal the sick, not those who were well. He came to preach to the Jews, not to the Gentiles. He took time away from the crowds instead of always tending to them.

Saying no can feel contrary to our deep desires for helping, serving, and being needed, but Jesus never modeled saying yes to everything!

Saying no can be loving to ourselves. Even Jesus did not have an infinite capacity to serve. He took time away from the crowd, even though people were hurting, sick, and in need. He took time alone to pray, even though people expected Him to teach and be among His followers.

Saying no reveals that we know our purpose and our worth. Saying no expresses that we need to focus our time and energy on other things. It's not that the thing we are saying no to is bad, but that we have other good things in our life that need our attention.

SHIFT IN FOCUS

Is there something in your life that you need to say no to? Perhaps it's a request from a friend or a commitment you found yourself involved in. Ask the Lord right now to give you a clear vision of what is yours to do: does this fit into it? Maybe you need to lovingly say no so that you can focus on what He has for you to do instead.

• • • • • • • • • • • **DAY 30**

Loving Boldly: Asking for Help Is Brave
By Christine Rollings

Fear not, for I am with you; be not dismayed, for I am your God;
I will strengthen you, I will help you,
I will uphold you with my righteous right hand.
(Isaiah 41:10)

Do you ever find yourself starting to pray, then fearing that it is too small a thing to ask from God? Do you find yourself wishing that your friend could see your need and step in to meet that need without you having to ask? It's true that not everyone has the ability to see a need and meet it like a Two can. What that means for us is this: we need to ask for help when we need it rather than wait on others to see it.

Dear Two, you are so aware of the needs around you. You are eager to offer help, even when it costs you. This is a powerful gift because it reflects God's desire and willingness to help us! But it is hard for us to ask for help from God and from others.

It takes vulnerability to ask for help. We must admit that we don't have it all together. How much I want to have it all together! How much I want to help others without needing their help! But my need is the very thing that makes me a part of the community that I'm in. It's this very thing, asking for help, that makes others more willing to allow me to help them as well.

When we ask for help, we declare our dependence on God and on those around us. We allow them to love us in a way we hear it the loudest.

SHIFT IN FOCUS

Asking for help starts with knowing where we need help. Sometimes that's the hardest part! We can get so used to doing it on our own that we don't see opportunities for inviting others into our lives in this way.

Take a moment to think about one way you can ask someone for help; it can be small task from God, a spouse, or a friend. Ask for help today and celebrate this brave act.

10 Days of Saying No to Manipulation
Help with a Common Pain Point

● ● ● ● ● ● ● ● ● ● ● **DAY 31**

What Is Manipulation?

*But understand this, that in the last days there will come times of
difficulty. For people will be lovers of self, lovers of money, proud,
arrogant, abusive, disobedient to their parents, ungrateful, unholy,
heartless, unappeasable, slanderous, without self-control, brutal,
not loving good, treacherous, reckless, swollen with conceit, lovers
of pleasure rather than lovers of God, having the appearance of
godliness, but denying its power. Avoid such people.*
(2 Timothy 3:1–5)

Manipulation is influencing events, thoughts, or behaviors
with your own words, thoughts, or behaviors without making
your motive or intentions clear. Manipulation is a form of mas-
terful trickery, and, unfortunately, those who use it feel it is altogether necessary.

Manipulation, over time, turns into a dangerous habit. You
may not realize that your little manipulative tendencies have
turned monstrous. Manipulation destroys relationships and
everything you try to build.

Manipulation is sneaky. Here are some examples of what it
can look like.

+ Manipulation can look like giving people options but being happy only when they pick the one you wanted, and then punishing them with your attitude.

+ Manipulation can look like lavishing people with gifts without verbalizing expectations for them to return the kindness.

+ Manipulation can look like telling the truth but not the whole truth.

+ Manipulation can look like exaggerating your emotions to elicit a specific response from others.

+ Manipulation can look like giving someone the silent treatment to get them to shower you with gifts and/or attention.

Manipulation feels powerful, necessary, natural, and effective to those who use it. Very often, it works, but at a cost. The cost of sin, the cost of truth, the cost of the relationships either now or in the future is great. The longer manipulation is used, the harder it can be to break; after all, if you don't want to plainly ask for what you want, you have to manipulate to get your needs met.

SHIFT IN FOCUS

Manipulation is a pretty dirty word in our culture, and it might've made you cringe to see it here. Or maybe you were fully expecting it, defense in hand for why this doesn't reflect you as a Two. We'll get to that tomorrow, but first, I want you to consider how manipulation from others has affected you. Have you ever been manipulated?

• • • • • • • • • • • • DAY 32

I Don't Do That. Yes, You Do

> *Do not be deceived: God is not mocked,*
> *for whatever one sows, that will he also reap.*
> (Galatians 6:7)

It's so hard to admit to manipulative behaviors. I know it may *feel* better not to acknowledge this part of being a Two, but believe me when I say with utmost kindness and firmness that this part of being a Two does, in one way or another, apply to you.

Manipulating other people often starts in childhood, which can make it all the harder to spot in adulthood. Did your parents ignore some of your needs? Did you feel unable, unequipped, or even bad if you demanded that a need be met? Well, this habitat often breeds manipulative behaviors into Twos at a young age.

Perhaps you couldn't, for some reason, voice your needs. You could hint at them or indirectly ask for them. Often these hints worked, and you learned that you didn't have to say what you needed in order to make a point.

+ Maybe you slammed a door to get your parents' attention or communicate your feelings.

+ Maybe you lied about your grades to get praise.

+ Maybe you pouted when your siblings got something you wanted.

+ Maybe you didn't say anything at the moment, but you punished your parents later by misbehaving.

- Maybe you said something like, "I guess you don't love me anymore?" or something else you knew would hit your parents right where it hurt.

- Maybe manipulation looked more like buttering your parents up, doing more chores than needed, complimenting them, or obeying in order to get that extra television time, praise, or sleepover.

This was manipulation. Children don't usually have the skills to work through their needs, others' responses, and their own worth. However, by the grace of Christ, you do. The problem is that the longer you cope using manipulation, the harder it is to believe that you can directly ask for what you need or want and it not end in relational flames.

Satan would love you to live your entire life without surrendering this part of yourself because it's sin. The more he can steal your peace, joy, and faithfulness here on earth, the better. That's what he wants. He is actively trying to steal your peace and tempt you away from joyful obedience.

If you can humbly see this part of yourself, then you are much more likely to surrender it to God. This should be our goal. Denial leads to burying this part of ourselves, and unrepentance abounds.

SHIFT IN FOCUS

Pray this prayer with me:

Dear heavenly Father, I pray that You would search my heart and reveal the places that are prone to the manipulation of others. Help me to notice, repent, and lean on You for change. Help me to walk humbly as I serve those around me. I want to love well, and I know You can help me do that. In Jesus's name, amen.

DAY 33 • • • • • • • • • •

Passive-Aggressive Tactics

Rather, speaking the truth in love, we are to grow up in every way into him who is the head, into Christ.
(Ephesians 4:15)

Passive aggression and manipulation often go hand in hand because the motivation for both is often very similar. Both manipulation (skillfully controlling a situation without being forthright) and passive aggression (resisting the demands of others and avoiding direct confrontation) are like saying, "I want my way, and I want you to know what I want. However, I'm not going to risk rejection, confrontation, or voicing my needs to get it."

People who are prone to manipulation often use passive-aggressive tendencies to make a point or say something without actually having to say it.

You may not sign a goodbye card at work because you're mad your friend is leaving and will be getting paid more. You're saying you're mad…but you're not actually saying it. Your husband came home late for the third time this week, so today, you didn't make dinner. You're saying you're upset, but you're not actually saying it. Your mom bought your sister a huge birthday present, but she only bought you a $25 gift card to the mall, so you pretend to be too busy to get your mom something for her birthday. You're getting revenge without saying a word.

Passive aggression is a form of lying. It is sin, and it never delivers on its promise. Passive aggression says, "You don't need to risk anything to make your point; you don't even have to say a word."

But the problem is that you *are* hurting someone, and it's very likely that the point you're trying to make is getting lost in translation. The other party doesn't get to voice his or her side. You're making a point to cover you, and it hurts someone else.

Passive aggression seeps out when you try too hard to shove your emotions down. Twos use repression as a defensive mechanism. Some of your feelings horrify you so much that you'd rather not admit you feel them. In fact, you'd rather hide them away where they'll never see the light of day and never hurt anyone. The problem is that repressed emotions still come out; they often come out sideways in the form of passive aggression.

Speaking the truth in love is the opposite of manipulation. Speaking the truth in love says, "I love you enough to be honest with you about my feelings or needs, even when I'm hurt."

Speaking the truth in love assumes that the other party wants reconciliation and a good relationship with you, which is true 95 percent of the time! We need to treat the people we love with honesty and believe that they want a good relationship just as much as we do. Passive aggression accomplishes none of these things.

SHIFT IN FOCUS

Passive-aggressive tendencies may or may not be obvious in your life. Regardless, you should be aware of what they look like and the harm they can cause.

+ Were you convicted of passive-aggressive behaviors as you read the examples?

+ Where do you need to speak the truth in love?

+ Is there an opportunity for this today?

• • • • • • • • • • • **DAY 34**

What the Bible Says About Manipulation
By Alison Bradley

*Love is patient and kind; love does not envy or boast;
it is not arrogant or rude. It does not insist on its own way;
it is not irritable or resentful; it does not rejoice at wrongdoing,
but rejoices with the truth.*
(1 Corinthians 13:4–6)

It can be such a difficult thing to identify manipulation in your life without a gauge outside of your own heart. The Bible may not use the word *manipulation*, but it is very clear about what real love looks like.

First Corinthians 13 may be a very familiar passage; even so, I encourage you to use Paul's words on love to evaluate your true motives. Before Paul speaks about what love looks like, he explains that sacrifice and giving aren't necessarily loving. "*If I give away all I have, and if I deliver up my body to be burned, but have not love, I gain nothing*" (1 Corinthians 13:3). These feel like the ultimate acts of love, don't they? But if a person's heart isn't loving, Paul minces no words—the acts are meaningless. How it looks on the outside makes no difference to God. He looks at our hearts.

Use this passage to examine your heart for any trace of manipulation. Let's look at some specific attributes of love.

"*Love does not envy or boast.*" Both envy and boasting involve looking at others, comparing what you are doing or what you have. Comparison has no place in love. When you act out of love, you do not measure what you do against what others do. You do not look to others as your gauge, to make yourself feel good. You remember that you answer to God alone for your actions. You aren't concerned about others, if they do more or less than you, or if you are being treated well enough. You care only about what God thinks about your heart, trusting Him to care for you.

"It does not insist on its own way." This one can be subtle. Real love doesn't insist on or punish others for not getting what it wants. Do you expect a return for what you've given? Do you pout or show your displeasure when things don't go your way? This is not a loving response; this is manipulative.

"It is not irritable or resentful." You may not feel irritable or resentful in the moment of giving or helping, but what if you receive nothing in return? Would that be okay with you? If you can't answer yes, you are setting yourself up for resentment and irritation with that person. Real love offers kindness without expecting anything in return.

Love *"rejoices with the truth."* How would you feel if someone didn't need your help? The truth can be a painful thing to hear. Love is grateful for the truth, even if it hurts or is costly. If you act in love, you won't trick people into doing what you want by omitting details or giving partial truths. You'll ask directly for what you want, and appreciate the truthful response you're given, surrendering any disappointment to the Lord.

Dear Two, these may be hard words to hear, but they are not meant to shame you. The Lord does not reveal our sin to shame or to guilt us. He loves you with the love described in 1

Corinthians 13; He is patient and kind, bearing and hoping all things for you.

SHIFT IN FOCUS

Read 1 Corinthians 13:1–7. Which verse about love stands out to you? Consider memorizing it or writing it on a card as a reminder as you seek to love others. Invite the Lord to reveal to you any tendency toward manipulation and be quick to repent when He reveals it.

DAY 35 • • • • • • • • • • •

How Jesus Handled Manipulation
By Alison Bradley

When he drew near and saw the city, he wept over it, saying, "Would that you, even you, had known on this day the things that make for peace! But now they are hidden from your eyes." (Luke 19:41–42)

Pause for a moment to read Luke 20:1–8:

One day, as Jesus was teaching the people in the temple and preaching the gospel, the chief priests and the scribes with the elders came up and said to him, "Tell us by what authority you do these things, or who it is that gave you this authority." He answered them, "I also will ask you a question. Now tell me, was the baptism of John from heaven or from man?" And they discussed it with one another, saying, "If we say, 'From heaven,' he will say, 'Why did you not believe him?' But if we say, 'From man,' all the people will stone us to death, for they are convinced that John was a prophet." So they answered that they did not know where it came from. And Jesus said to them, "Neither will I tell you by what authority I do these things."

Instead of asking Jesus directly for what they wanted to know, the priests and scribes tried to manipulate Him to reveal what they wanted. Jesus didn't directly answer their questions but questioned them in return. When they failed to answer Him, Jesus also refused to answer their questions.

It can feel tempting when we're on the receiving end of manipulation to play the game, just to give the other person what they want. But Jesus showed us that the most loving thing to do is to set boundaries and not participate at all. Jesus knew their hearts and discerned what would be wise and helpful. He knew that going along with their scheme would not yield a productive or loving conversation. Instead, He showed them love by asking them to evaluate their own hearts. He showed them love by not giving them what they wanted.

From the other side of this manipulation encounter, it can be hard to receive this kind of love. It can be hard to see love when someone isn't giving you what you want. But notice what Jesus did in the previous chapter. He wept over Jerusalem.

Imagine this scene. Jesus saw Jerusalem in the distance, and He was overcome with emotion. I can't help but believe that He was thinking of real people: the people He loved, including those whose hearts were still trying to manipulate to get what they wanted. Jesus may have been angry over the harm they were doing to others (He cleansed the temple in the following passage), but you can see the love He was showing here. With Jesus, anger and grief are expressions of His love. And He grieves when you are blind to the things that would bring you true connection and healing.

SHIFT IN FOCUS

Jesus always acts out of love and models how to do so for us, even in the messy area of manipulation.

If today's passage reminded you of times that you've been manipulated, pause and consider Jesus's example of not entering into unproductive conversations or unhelpful actions. You might not be able to see someone else's heart, but you have the Holy Spirit to offer you guidance and help in the moment. What would it look like for you to set these kinds of boundaries in the future? Ask the Lord to help you to have the courage to say no, with love.

If today's passage felt convicting (perhaps for the times you've been manipulative), remember that you are loved. Ask the Lord to help you trust that there is love behind any "no" He might give, including the boundaries others might set with you. Invite Him to help you believe that you are loved, even when you may not get what you want. Ask Him to show you how He sees you, revealing your sin for what it is and reassuring you of His love.

• • • • • • • • • • • **DAY 36**

Giving with Strings Attached Is Not Kind
By Christine Rollings

Love is patient and kind; love does not envy or boast;
it is not arrogant or rude. It does not insist on its own way;
it is not irritable or resentful.
(1 Corinthians 13:4–5)

Dear Two, have you ever given with strings attached? Have you considered that this type of giving could be a form of manipulation? I had not seen this in myself until I learned about the Enneagram.

I had moved to a new city and was just getting to know the people in my community. I felt lonely and wondered what it would take for me to make the kinds of friends you could give a spare key to or ask to water your plants when you're away. When I learned that a new friend was sick, I jumped on the opportunity to make a meal. I felt proud of myself for seeing a need and knowing how to meet it. But I considered a new insight I had recently learned from the Enneagram: was I trying to get something out of this?

I saw it right away: I gave so that I could ask for help later. I was storing up favors, keeping track in my mind.

This is not kind. This is giving to get something. This is manipulation. Catching myself in this type of giving, I prayed as I made the meal, "Father, help me expect nothing in return from this gift. Let this be a love offering to You and my new friend. Give me joy in giving with no strings attached."

Kindness to others means giving with no expectation of return. Kindness means we don't give to get. Kindness does not keep score.

The gift itself is not wrong, so you are free to still give it, but not if you can't first release your expectations for a return. Your friends, family, and coworkers would likely prefer no gift rather than a gift with unknown stipulations and expectations attached to it.

SHIFT IN FOCUS

Think of a time when you've recently given something. Maybe it was a tangible gift or your time or emotional energy. Did you keep track of that gift? *If I give this, then I can ask for something later. If I accept this help, I need to make up for it later.* Consider what it would mean to give with kindness, asking and expecting nothing in return, not keeping track of your giving in your mind.

• • • • • • • • • • • • **DAY 37**

Giving with Strings Attached Is Not Generous
By Alison Bradley

Whoever sows sparingly will also reap sparingly, and whoever sows bountifully will also reap bountifully. Each one must give as he has decided in his heart, not reluctantly or under compulsion, for God loves a cheerful giver. And God is able to make all grace abound to you, so that having all sufficiency in all things at all times, you may abound in every good work.
(2 Corinthians 9:6–8)

It can be hard to look at your own heart, considering the real reasons you give to others. Pay attention to your motivations for giving and see if there are any strings attached. Paul offered some practical help in evaluating your own heart in 2 Corinthians 9.

He said you get to decide what you give. This should not be determined by what others do, by external pressure, or by an expectation for reciprocation. This should be decided between you and the Lord. You are invited to consider what the Lord might have for you to give, trusting that He will provide for that giving as well as for your needs. You will be taken care of, even as you give without strings attached. The Lord will supply all we need to be generous and partner with Him to care for others.

"*Not reluctantly or under compulsion*" (2 Corinthians 9:7) is such a helpful gauge for giving. Is there any hint of reluctance or obligation in what you are doing? Are you expecting something in return for this giving? We can look to Jesus as our model for how to give. He didn't wash the disciples' feet and expect them to do something for Him in return. He didn't quietly resent the needs of those He healed. He gave of Himself because He wanted to. And when *He* had a need, He asked for help directly, such as when He asked the disciples to stay awake with Him in the garden. His request was not tied to what He had given in the past.

"For God loves a cheerful giver" (2 Corinthians 9:7). In the past when I heard this verse, I would feel guilty for all the times I haven't given cheerfully, or when I felt pressure to put on a fake smile when I gave. But that wasn't what Paul was talking about at all! He was talking about the joy the Lord receives when others reflect His own joy in giving. Paul reminds us of the Lord's generous heart toward us, making *"all grace abound"* to us (verse 8) and being *"enriched in every way to be generous in every way"* (verse 11.) We see the ultimate generous act in Jesus Himself, giving up everything so that we could be made right with God. Jesus gave freely and gladly, with no strings attached, for us to receive Him.

SHIFT IN FOCUS

What stood out to you about the passage? Did the Lord reveal anything to your heart? If so, pause and talk to the Lord about what He showed you today.

As you consider if there are strings attached to your giving, be encouraged that the Lord has given you what you need to be generous like He is generous. Pause to read and celebrate the truth of 2 Corinthians 9:10–11: *"He who supplies seed to the sower and bread for food will supply and multiply your seed for sowing and increase the harvest of your righteousness. You will be enriched in every way to be generous in every way."*

DAY 38 • • • • • • • • •

Giving with Strings Attached Is Not Godly
By Christine Rollings

God loves a cheerful giver.
(2 Corinthians 9:7)

Your awareness of needs around you, your helpful spirit, and your generous heart all reflect God. Others see God's heart when you give without strings attached, showing His abundant love and generosity.

When we keep a record of our giving and expect to get something in return, we aren't showing the heart of God. I'm reminded of this as I consider God's gift of Jesus to us: *"But God shows his love for us in that while we were still sinners, Christ died for us"* (Romans 5:8).

"While we were still sinners"—that's key for me. While I wasn't interested in knowing Him. While I wasn't walking in the light of His goodness and truth. While I was trying to live life on my own. Christ didn't die for me because I was worthy of receiving this gift. He didn't die for me so that I would feel obligated to receive His forgiveness. God showed His love for me by selflessly making a way for us to know Him.

We long for God's love to flow through us to those around us. His love is pure, not manipulative, offering us freedom of will and choice. His love gives us the freedom to say no. His love even gives us the freedom to hurt Him.

This love is hard to give, but a gift to receive. This love has no strings attached, offering freedom to the recipient. It's making that meal and not even expecting to get the dish back. It's moving toward a child who is rebelling against your love.

Cut those strings, dear Two, and watch the love of God soar in your life.

SHIFT IN FOCUS

How has God been generous toward you? We can learn to be abundant in our generosity by seeing how He has been generous toward us.

DAY 39 • • • • • • • • • • •

Gifting Awareness

*Beware of practicing your righteousness before other people in order
to be seen by them, for then you will have no reward from your
Father who is in heaven. Thus, when you give to the needy,
sound no trumpet before you, as the hypocrites do in the synagogues
and in the streets, that they may be praised by others.
Truly, I say to you, they have received their reward. But when you
give to the needy, do not let your left hand know what your right
hand is doing, so that your giving may be in secret.
And your Father who sees in secret will reward you.*
(Matthew 6:1–4)

Now maybe you're convicted of this in your life but you are
still struggling to see it play out as it happens. Most of us aren't
aware we are giving with strings attached or expectations in the
moment, but months or years later, that sickening feeling hits us.

"I gave Mary a huge gift basket when she retired, and she
couldn't even be bothered to show up to my retirement party." Or, "I
asked Joe to be a groomsman in my wedding, but he didn't have me
in his wedding at all!" This is keeping a record of what you're giving.
That gift wasn't so much a thought of generosity as a contract.

I think most of us know that this isn't right; it's a pretty ugly
feeling when we feel like someone hasn't met his end of the bar-
gain we had set up for him, but what do we do?

Matthew 6:1 says, *"Beware,"* which means to be cautiously alert. If you're aware this is a problem for you, then you need to be ahead of the game.

Would you feel uncomfortable if you didn't sign your name on this card? What if you left this gift on their porch? Or what if you chose to be anonymous for an online monetary gift? If those things make you uncomfortable, I'd suggest asking yourself a continuous string of *why* questions to flesh it out.

What's the worst that could happen? They'd have no one to thank? Would they have to thank God? Isn't that what the goal of generosity should be, to point others to our generous God?

Of course, every gift doesn't need to be given anonymously, but if you struggle with manipulation in this way, maybe it needs to start becoming an option for you. Just some food for thought.

SHIFT IN FOCUS

Do you need more gifting awareness in your life? Pray and ask God to help you beware of how you give and to give with a generous heart.

DAY 40 • • • • • • • • • • • •

Stop, Ask, and Give

But test everything; hold fast what is good.
(1 Thessalonians 5:21)

Beware (or being aware) is what God calls us to do in this area of our lives, especially if we battle manipulative and prideful giving.

A useful exercise that has served my clients as well as my own heart over the years is this: stop, ask, and give.

Stop

Before you give, take a moment to stop. Maybe this will occur in a store while picking out a gift, while you're making a gift, or while you're wrapping a gift. Pick one moment that you'll remember and stop.

Ask

Ask yourself this simple yet tough question: "Will I feel okay if I don't get anything in return for this gift?" Not a thank-you, not a kind gesture, not even a *feeling* of more affection toward you. Nothing in return. If you can't say, "Yes, I will be okay if I get nothing in return," then you should not give the gift. This may feel a little shocking in the moment. Here are your options:

- Asking for a change of heart. Pray and ask God to change your heart. Pray for the recipient, that he or she would feel God's generosity through this gift and not even remember the giver.

✦ Giving the gift anyway and resenting the recipient later. If that person forgets or simply doesn't repay the gift, then you might start to feel bitter. If this is the case, it would be kinder for you not to give a gift at all.

If you can give the gift with no strings attached, or experience a heart change before you give, then you can move on to the last step.

Give

Give with a generous, non-record-keeping heart. It's the best for all parties involved. The kindness of giving is not worth bitterness building up in a relationship and the potential of sinning. It's not worth it—period!

SHIFT IN FOCUS

Can you think of a moment that would be a helpful *stop sign* for you? How can you use this exercise in the future?

_____

_____

10 Days Of Handling Anger
Going To Eight in Stress

• • • • • • • • • • • DAY 41
Seasons of Life

For everything there is a season, and a time for every matter under heaven: a time to be born, and a time to die; a time to plant, and a time to pluck up what is planted; a time to kill, and a time to heal; a time to break down, and a time to build up; a time to weep, and a time to laugh; a time to mourn, and a time to dance; a time to cast away stones, and a time to gather stones together; a time to embrace, and a time to refrain from embracing; a time to seek, and a time to lose; a time to keep, and a time to cast away; a time to tear, and a time to sew; a time to keep silence, and a time to speak; a time to love, and a time to hate; a time for war, and a time for peace.
(Ecclesiastes 3:1–8)

In the whirlwind of life, expectations, and demands, it can be hard to think of ourselves as living seasonally. We live on an earth with winter, spring, summer, and fall, and we observe and celebrate the earth and its seasons, but we rarely give ourselves permission to change and transform. Instead, we expect all or nothing. Either I am...or I am not. There is right now, and anything worth doing is worth doing today. This is especially true in the hustle of America.

Of course, as we look at our own life, seasons are evident. There was that really hard year of illness, there were years of singleness, there were those amazing three months of falling in love, there were years with little kids, there were years of learning—everything in its own season.

We have a lot to learn from the way God created the earth with its seasons. In Ecclesiastes 3:1–8, we read that there is a season for everything and we know that this is about us, not just the earth. For every bad and hard season, there was a season of rest and good to come.

SHIFT IN FOCUS

In the next nine days, we will go into detail about what seasons of stress look like for you as a Two.

As you look at your own life today, what season are you in? Read Ecclesiastes 3:1–8 again and pick one or two adjectives that represent the season you're in. Are you mourning or celebrating? Transitioning or resting? Uprooting or planting?

If you're in a more hopeful, joyful, and restful season, it may be time to press into growth and celebrate the growth you can see in yourself. If you're in a season of hard transition and survival, it may be helpful for you to view this time as a passing season and discover hope on the horizon. You may see some ways that you're growing even in stress and adversity. Celebrate those wins!

• • • • • • • • • • • DAY 42

What Is a Season of Stress?

I can't get it to work:

Cast your burden on the LORD, and he will sustain you;
he will never permit the righteous to be moved.
(Psalm 55:22)

In talking about the seasons of life, we all know that there are seasons of great stress.

When we talk about stress using Enneagram verbiage, we aren't talking about the being-late-for-work kind of stress. We all get frustrated and irritable in such circumstances. No, when the Enneagram refers to stress, it means seasonal stress, such as losing a job, transitioning, losing a loved one, and so forth. In those times, we're in survival mode, often for months or years. These are the seasons of stress we are talking about.

During seasons of stress, Twos might become more agitated, reactive, and combative than normal. Perhaps you feel angrier, although you may say you are *frustrated* or *irritated*. All of a sudden, everyone expects something of you, and you've had it. You may have an urge to control your environment and what's happening with detailed precision. This is the reality of a stressed-out Two.

These behaviors should signal you to stop and ask yourself a few questions:

+ What is stressing me out right now?

+ Am I in a season of stress?

+ If I could look back on myself in this season of stress, how may I have been kinder to the people in my life?

+ Where should I be resting or giving myself more grace in this season?

We should not be ashamed of seasons of stress. If anything, they move us to cling to God in a precious way and to become more aware of our need for Him.

SHIFT IN FOCUS

Take a couple of moments to reflect on the season you're in right now. Is this a season of growth or a season of stress?

If it's a season of stress, take a deep breath, be kind to your battered heart, and cling to your Savior.

• • • • • • • • • • • **DAY 43**

How Do I Go to Eight in Stress?

> *When the sun rose, God appointed a scorching east wind,*
> *and the sun beat down on the head of Jonah so that he was faint.*
> *And he asked that he might die and said, "It is better for me to die*
> *than to live." But God said to Jonah, "Do you do well to be*
> *angry for the plant?" And he said, "Yes, I do well to be angry,*
> *angry enough to die."*
> (Jonah 4:8–9)

The realities of going to Eight in stress aren't as easily described as they are felt. Being an Enneagram Two is like having a volcano living dormant in your chest at all times. When you go through a stressful season of life, it starts to become active. It might take a little while before it is fully spewing lava all over your life, but you are probably familiar with the rumble of its awakening.

The Rumble

An awakening volcano is best described as agitation. You may get easily irritated, which is exacerbated when others notice and mention it. This may happen without a full-fledged season of stress, such as when you have a week or day of stress, but it is a warning signal nonetheless. Stop, pray, and ask yourself what is really going on. Why are you stressed?

The Awakening

An awakening volcano looks more like a sporadic spout of anger. You may yell at your kids in the car, stomp away, slam a door, or throw something. The volcano has awakened and started showing itself on the outside. This is a bigger warning that you need to stop and give yourself some time to figure out what's going on in your heart and life.

The Disaster

Active volcanoes leave wreckage in their paths. You may scream, fight, say things you don't mean, and be overly hostile and mean. If this happens, immediate humility and repentance are of paramount importance. There is more going on than these behaviors; you're likely struggling to keep everything together, and this anger is a symptom of deeper things.

Jonah got angry when the plant that was shading him withered away. (See Jonah 4:6–7.) When we are stressed, we may get angry over little things that are not the real problem. What are we really stressed about? What action can we take to help ourselves through this season? What do we need to give to God?

SHIFT IN FOCUS

Are you in a season of stress right now? Which stage of volcanic activity are you witnessing?

• • • • • • • • • • • **DAY 44**

The Struggles of Type Eight

Learn to do good; seek justice, correct oppression;
bring justice to the fatherless, plead the widow's cause.
(Isaiah 1:17)

I once had a client ask me, "Why does going to Eight in stress manifest as anger? That can't be all Eights are."

I think this is a brilliant question because it gets at a much deeper truth. Anger, frustration, and irritation all are loud byproducts of an Eight's main motivation of autonomy being triggered, the idea that "I must not be controlled."

Eights are not merely angry people, despite being part of the gut triad. They're zealous people, tenderhearted people, hard-working and passionate people. They're strong and fierce on the outside because they're protective and very compassionate. They love deeply—and it just so happens that one of the costs of loving deeply is fiercely defending your people. If you cross someone who is loved by an Eight, you'll feel it. Isaiah 1:17 is a *life verse* of type Eights. They have a lot of energy, they don't like to waste time, and they're focused on the future. They're often a big voice for the voiceless and leaders in social justice of all kinds.

Why should you know all of this? Because by learning more about Eights, you're learning about yourself, and what stress may look like for you.

When you go to an Eight in stress, you enter into a fight for control, the battleground that Eights live in. Seasons of stress are often out of our control and being out of control causes a lot of anxiety. This lack of control makes Twos try even harder to regain what has been threatened.

This is what it can look like:

+ Irritation – "This isn't going my way."

+ Frustration – "I'm losing control."

+ Anger – "I've lost control."

SHIFT IN FOCUS

Can you see a fight for control behind your stress symptoms? Think about a recent stressful time. What felt out of your control?

• • • • • • • • • • • • DAY 45

The Temptation of Anger
By Christine Rollings

Know this, my beloved brothers: let every person be quick to hear,
slow to speak, slow to anger; for the anger of man
does not produce the righteousness of God.
(James 1:19–20)

How might the temptation of anger in stress manifest in your life?

You may yell at a friend, spouse, or child. You may stop talking to someone, or you may quietly let your anger simmer in your heart until it comes out in small ways like a slammed door, a snide comment, or some other passive-aggressive behavior. None of these reactions are the fruits of the righteousness of God.

The first step toward growth when we are tempted with these behaviors is admitting that we feel angry. Not frustrated, not irritated—angry. Sometimes, the first sign that I am moving toward anger is when I tell myself, "I'm so frustrated!" This is when I need to check my heart. This is when I may be able to save the village from volcanic eruption!

In these moments, I pause and ask myself these questions:

+ What is causing my anger?

+ What kind of control am I longing for here?

+ How can I release this need for control in this moment?

Here's an example:

What is causing my anger? My baby keeps waking up at night.

What kind of control am I longing for here? I want to be able to control how much sleep I get at night.

How can I release this need for control in this moment? I need to remember that she's a baby and that this is a season right now. (Remind myself of truth.) I can make sure I go to bed early to maximize my sleep. (Take control of what I *can* control.) I can ask God to help me on those sleepless nights. (Ask for His presence and acknowledge that He is with me even in my anger.)

Instead of taking my anger out on my baby or my husband, I can speak truth to my heart and ask God to help me. Now, this doesn't naturally happen in moments of anger for me. Often, it happens as I reflect on it later, and I regularly need to apologize to those around me. But the more I reflect and ask myself these questions, the more I am aware of my need for control and my propensity toward anger, and the more I can repent and grow. This is how you become slow to anger.

Here's the thing, dear Two: anger isn't always bad. Anger is an emotion. And while it may feel safer to discount anger altogether, labeling it as a bad emotion, the Bible doesn't do that. James said to be *"slow to anger."* He didn't say to never feel anger. Being slow to anger means that our anger rarely comes to the surface, but the goal here isn't to discount and repress it. We need to listen to what our anger is telling us about our reality and use it as a tool instead of a weapon.

SHIFT IN FOCUS

What signs reveal that you are angry? Do you notice it before it comes bubbling out like lava, or do you see it when confronted with your behavior? List a few ways you see anger start to simmer in your heart:

_____

_____

The next time you notice one of these simmer points, ask yourself the questions previously discussed.

DAY 46 • • • • • • • • • • •

The Temptation of Control
By Christine Rollings

Where were you when I laid the foundation of the earth?
Tell me, if you have understanding.
(Job 38:4)

Most days, I want my life to be predictable. When I am in seasons of stress, when I feel as if I'm on the Tilt-A-Whirl ride at the carnival, I want to not only hold on to the rail, but also stop the ride altogether. I want to be able to push a button and get off.

Early in our marriage, my husband and I spent two years living in Manila, Philippines. Our time living in this city of nearly twenty million people, with traffic and pollution, was a season of stress for me, and my desire to control was strong.

One time, as we flew back to our home in Manila after visiting family, I made lists. I made lists of what my daily routine could look like. I made lists of things I could do while I waited in traffic or in line at the grocery store. I made lists for other lists. As I sat there on a layover, sharing my projected coping strategy with my husband, I felt as if I was preparing for battle.

After hearing my plan, he responded, "It sounds like you are grasping for control."

I pushed back, explaining that I needed my lists because they helped and comforted me. Yet as I talked, I realized he was right.

I needed control. I needed to feel like I could control *something* in the midst of the traffic, the crowds, and the intense heat.

It's true that we can control ourselves and our responses, but this is even harder during seasons of stress. When Twos are under stress, they often feel anger about things they can't control and attempt to control whatever they can.

In Job 38, God responded to Job's lament over his grief and season of stress. He put Job in his place: "Are you God? No, you are not."

Maybe in stressful seasons, you attempt to control your surroundings, making sure things go your way. Maybe in stressful seasons, you attempt to control the people in your life, hoping to grasp stability in your relationships. When we try to control, we try to play God. We want to know what's coming, and we want it to go our way. But God puts us in our place: "Are you God? No, you are not."

SHIFT IN FOCUS

Read God's response to Job in chapter 38.

How can understanding our place before God help us handle our temptation to control?

DAY 47 • • • • • • • • • • •

The Temptation of Manipulative Punishment
By Christine Rollings

Let what you say be simply "Yes" or "No";
anything more than this comes from evil.
(Matthew 5:37)

Manipulation feels like such a dirty word, especially when we have been victims of manipulation in the past. We know that being manipulated feels confusing, painful, and infuriating. It feels like the very opposite of love.

Manipulation is self-serving; it is a person's attempt to control the world and the people around them. In seasons of stress, this is one of our go-to's in getting what we want.

Even on days we feel like we have margin and space in our souls, it feels hard to name what we need and harder still to ask for it. When we go to Eight in stress, that gets even harder. In order to get what we need, often without realizing it, we try to manipulate others into giving us what we want without asking.

Instead of saying, "I am angry," I will slam the door on the way out of my room so my spouse knows that I'm angry.

Instead of saying, "I need encouragement," I will wallow in self-pity with a friend.

Instead of taking steps to restore a relationship, I will offer the silent treatment until the other person pursues me and admit his or her wrongs.

Dear Two, this isn't the way of love. In the moment, it feels like the safer option because we do not have to figure out or speak our needs. We try to control our friend, spouse, or child into giving us the response that we want. But this is not a loving relationship.

In His Sermon on the Mount, Jesus spoke to our honesty in the context of taking oaths. (See Matthew 5:33–37.) He reminded us that we don't need to swear on anything, as our words should be exactly what we mean. A yes and a no should be spoken as a yes and a no.

This is how we need to learn to speak our needs: when we're angry, we must say that we are angry. When we are hurting, we must speak up for that too, not just offer silence and hope that the other person figures it out.

SHIFT IN FOCUS

Does manipulation become even more of a temptation for you in seasons of stress? Can you think of a time that you used manipulation to get what you want? Doing this can feel so natural that often we don't even notice we're doing it until we're confronted later. Consider the examples given for this day and think of what it may look like for you. Even if you are not currently in a season of stress, make a plan now for what you can do differently the next time you are tempted to punish someone in this way.

DAY 48 • • • • • • • • • •

When You're Tempted to Discount Your Anger

If we confess our sins, he is faithful and just to forgive us our sins and to cleanse us from all unrighteousness.
(1 John 1:9)

Discounting anger is very natural for most Twos. Anger feels bad or scary. Being angry feels as if we are out of control and need to seek help. In American culture, anger is not seen as neutral. Anger can have many forms, some of which are good and righteous, but we view anger as just *bad*. We think that if we're angry, then we're out of control.

So how do we discount anger? We say, "Oh, I was just frustrated," "I'm getting really irritated," or "I'm not angry, I'm just tired (or fill in the blank)."

What would happen if we called anger what it is? Does the very thought of that make you squirm a little in your seat? Probably. Because you don't want to be a bad person. Believe me, I get it, but isn't lying about how you're really feeling equally as bad?

How would it make you feel to own up to your anger? This may look like saying, "I'm sorry I was angry," "I gave in to my anger, and that was wrong," or "I probably need to go cool off because I feel angry." Would others think less of you? I bet you they wouldn't. It takes a lot of humility to own up to sin and to be self-aware enough to know when you're about to mess up. People often admire, not judge, this type of honesty. It might even convict them of needing to be more honest themselves.

If you gave the people in your life this vulnerable outlook of what having a dormant volcano in your chest really looks like, they'd be better able to pray for you and be there for you. Half-truths promise something only honesty can deliver. They may buy you time, or maybe a momentary peace, but they don't bring you closer to Jesus.

SHIFT IN FOCUS

If you're stressed and fighting for control, you might try to find it by saying, "I'm not an angry person," or by discounting what you're feeling altogether. Perhaps you're telling yourself, "Maybe it'll go away," or "That was the last time I'll raise my voice in anger."

The problem is that, as with pride, using gentler words such as *frustrated* or *irritated* discounts our sin in our own eyes. Instead of acknowledging your anger as sin, you discount it to a mild feeling that can be fixed with a glass of wine or your version of a time-out.

Are you discounting your anger? If helpful, borrow these words of prayer:

Dear heavenly Father, I often feel anger, and I discount it with milder words. Would You convict me of this, even as it's happening? Please help me to be honest. Help me to run to You. Help me to trust that You are big enough to handle the truth of my anger, and You're eager to break the chains that tie me to it. Thank You for Your forgiving grace and for Your never-ending love for me. Amen.

• • • • • • • • • • • **DAY 49**

Acknowledging the Problem

> *Be strong and courageous. Do not fear or be in dread of them,*
> *for it is the LORD your God who goes with you.*
> *He will not leave you or forsake you.*
> *(Deuteronomy 31:6)*

Dear Two, are you honest about your stress? Do you know what has caused it? Is there something in your life that feels suffocating? If you're in a season of stress, list a couple of these things here:

1. _____

2. _____

Do you feel out of control? Do these things feel too big, too much, or too complicated? Are there any steps you can take to help your situation?

Then how can you survive this time? Can you spend more time in God's Word, play an audio Bible in the car, wake up earlier to make sure you have time with God, join a Bible study for some accountability, take a nap, take a couple of responsibilities off your plate for this season?

If you can, I'd encourage you to do so. Don't treat yourself like you're in a season of growth. You're surviving. How would a future you view you now? Would he or she wish you had done more? No! Future you will probably just be amazed that you got dressed and ate during this season. There are times and seasons for productivity and hospitality. Now just might not be that time. It's okay to say this; it's not something to feel guilty about. You're not doing anything wrong; you're simply surviving.

I'm giving you permission right now to take that step. Is it a phone call? Is it signing up for college classes? Is it a really hard conversation?

Dear Two, God is with you. You do not walk alone. He is ever near and ever faithful. Pray, breathe, and take the step.

This situation and how you react in stress can feel like chains or a volcano you have no control over. However, God is a chain breaker; He is the volcano creator and tamer. He can give you the freedom to not react in anger but to respond through the power of the Holy Spirit. He will lead you out of this, and He will never leave you, not for one second.

SHIFT IN FOCUS

Think about your answers to the questions for this day. What's one thing you can take off your plate? What's your next step?

• • • • • • • • • • • **DAY 50**

Surviving Without Blowing Up

The LORD is merciful and gracious, slow to anger
and abounding in steadfast love.
(Psalm 103:8)

If you're in a season of stress, and you feel your anger growing as if the volcano is about to erupt, you may feel desperate for help, desperate for some sense of control or normality. Believe me, we've all been there, no matter how put together someone's life seems.

Here is a list of things to try so you don't blow up while you're surviving:

1. Respond, don't react. In between being triggered and reacting in anger, there is always a moment of choice. You can choose to react or to walk away. You can choose to blow up or to take ten deep breaths. It may feel impossible in a moment of anger, so try it now. Ten deep breaths. In through your nose, out through your mouth. You won't look as ridiculous doing this as you would flying off the handle.

Here are some good actions to take after being triggered:

+ Take a walk.
+ Take ten deep breaths.
+ Take a shower.
+ Go to the gym.
+ Scream into a pillow.

+ Sit alone with your back against a wall and pray.
+ Listen to music while walking, taking a shower, or exercising.
+ Color, draw, or create something else with your hands.

2. Respond later. You can always revisit an issue later. It will still be there. You might even be amazed how much clearer you can see the problem if you distance yourself from the immediate emotion of it all.

3. Respond honestly. After the immediate anger of the moment has dissipated, be honest about how the situation or comment made you feel. If you need to apologize, do so, but as painful as it may be, don't pretend it was not a big deal or didn't happen.

4. Respond with grace. Do this both for yourself and for those around you. God is not only slow to anger but abounds in love. (See Psalm 103:8.) We need to find our example in Him, being slow to anger and abounding in love. Remind yourself of His grace and love for you, as this will help you give it to others as well.

SHIFT IN FOCUS

Which of these steps is hardest for you? Which step can you implement right now?

10 Days of Digging into Creativity and Emotional Honesty
Going to Four in Growth

● ● ● ● ● ● ● ● ● ● ● **DAY 51**

Seasons of Growth

*Every good gift and every perfect gift is from above, coming down
from the Father of lights, with whom there is no variation or
shadow due to change.*
(James 1:17)

Thinking of your life in seasonal terms is not only biblical, but it
also gives you a lot more grace and hope for your circumstances.
Seasons of stress are the opposite of seasons of *growth*. The latter
are periods in your life in which you feel as if you have room to
breathe, have more energy, and can focus on spiritual, mental,
and physical growth.

Seasons of growth are often blurry or over-romanticized
when we look back at our life as a whole. We either can't remember a time in our life that we didn't feel the hum of anxiety and
stress, or we can't live fully in the present because no season will
ever be as good as it has been in the past.

Both of these thought processes are unfruitful because
they're extremes. There is always a mixture of good and bad in
every situation; only the details change. This is a result of living

in a fallen world. We are living outside of our natural habitat, and it often feels like a paradox of good and bad at the same time.

Now, this doesn't mean that seasons of stress and growth coexist all the time; often, they don't. Circumstances in our lives often tip the scales. Nothing is ever *all bad* or *all good*. Working in a toxic environment or the death of a loved one will send us into a season of stress. Likewise, getting our dream job, hitting a sweet spot with parenting, or flourishing in a good friendship can tip the scale to seasons of growth.

During seasons of growth, we should push ourselves. Have you wanted to read a certain book or join a Bible study? Do it! Have you been waiting to start a diet or go to the gym? Now is the time! We literally have more mental space, more energy, and more bandwidth when we are in seasons of growth.

In seasons of growth, we can also see and build a lot of encouraging behaviors. Press into these behaviors and nurture them so that they'll stick beyond this season. Create good habits that will help in future stressful times. Consistent Bible reading is a must for all of life, but especially in those stressed-out days when we feel lost.

Growth seasons are the days of digging deep and reaping rewards. These seasons are gifts from a heavenly Father who loves us and wants to give us good things.

We should be using these seasons of good gifts to not only build up our faith but also to help others. (See 1 Peter 4:10.) In the next nine days, we'll see how going to the number Four in growth helps Twos to build up themselves and others.

SHIFT IN FOCUS

Are you currently in a season of growth?

Are there a couple of good seasons in your past that you may be over-romanticizing or may be ungrateful for?

DAY 52 • • • • • • • • • • • •

The Best of Type Four

And I am sure of this, that he who began a good work in you will bring it to completion at the day of Jesus Christ.
(Philippians 1:6)

The Enneagram teaches us that as Twos grow and become healthier, they pick up the positive qualities of type Four. You will find that as you feel more comfortable in the world, and as you trust what God says about your worth and value, it'll be easier for you to access your emotions, to express instead of repress these emotions. You'll have more access to your creative side and generate space to listen to others without feeling the need to help.

You'll see these qualities in abundance in seasons of growth, but that doesn't mean you can't plant seeds or seek out these qualities in other seasons.

As an overview, Type Fours are romantic individualists. They're deep people who don't push away their emotions like many others do. They crave authenticity, and they add uniquely to the world around them. They tend to be creative and thrive in beautiful and aesthetic environments.

If you know a couple of Fours personally, you may be a little repulsed by their seeming self-focus and abundant emotions. They may not seem to think of other people as you do, and you might not be attracted to the idea of becoming like them. Well, first off, the Fours who are the most obvious to you may be unhealthy, and when we are talking about growth numbers, we are talking about taking on the *best* qualities of Fours. If you can take a step back and see the positive qualities of the Fours in your life, or even just Fours in fiction, you'll find something your soul is drawn toward.

This includes emotional awareness, creative depth, empathy, an ability to see beauty in the world, ease in understanding themselves, and a slower pace to life.

SHIFT IN FOCUS

When was the last time you were in a season of growth? What creative pursuits did you enjoy in that season? Are there ways you can revisit or adopt that passion now?

DAY 53 • • • • • • • • • • •

How Do We Go to Four in Growth?

For his invisible attributes, namely, his eternal power and divine nature, have been clearly perceived, ever since the creation of the world, in the things that have been made. So they are without excuse. (Romans 1:20)

Going to Four in growth doesn't mean that you turn into a type Four but that you gain some of the positive strengths of Fours.

Fours tend to have a love of beauty that translates into being creative. Creative expression will look different for each Four, but it is fair to assume that quite a few Fours are famous musicians, artists, photographers, and writers. Creativity is one of the ways that Fours look at our Creator God and say, "I want to be like You."

In learning about type Four, you're learning about a very good part of yourself, and this is probably something you're vaguely aware of and access regularly. God knows what's good for us, and He can be trusted to lead us to those green pastures. (See Psalm 23:2.)

Do you feel closer to God when you walk in the woods or watch a colorful sunset? Admiring beauty and appreciating God's creation are marks of your growth.

You will probably feel less angst when you have some creative outlet because creativity is a way you can go to a Four in growth and the peace that comes with it.

When you're aware of an emotional need and speak it instead of repress it, don't you feel lighter? You may not feel this right away, but perhaps you do in the long run.

These all are ways you practically access Four, and you'll be doing it much more often in seasons of growth. That's how this works practically. Growing as a Two isn't a mystical concept; it's probably something you're already experiencing.

SHIFT IN FOCUS

Take a moment to read these verses:

And he has filled him with the Spirit of God, with skill, with intelligence, with knowledge, and with all craftsmanship, to devise artistic designs, to work in gold and silver and bronze.   (Exodus 35:31–32)

Be filled with the Spirit, addressing one another in psalms and hymns and spiritual songs, singing and making melody to the Lord with your heart.   (Ephesians 5:18–19)

What traits of Fours can you find in these verses?

DAY 54 • • • • • • • • • • •

Growing in Emotional Honesty
By Christine Rollings

O LORD, you have searched me and known me! You know when
I sit down and when I rise up; you discern my thoughts from afar.
You search out my path and my lying down and are acquainted with
all my ways. Even before a word is on my tongue, behold, O LORD,
you know it altogether. You hem me in, behind and before, and lay
your hand upon me. Such knowledge is too wonderful for me; it is
high; I cannot attain it.
(Psalm 139:1–6)

I don't consider myself to be a good liar. My mom tells me that growing up, I wouldn't even try to lie about something I did wrong. I'd confess to her right away and punish myself! Even keeping good surprises for the people I love is hard. One year, I felt so guilty for lying to my dad to keep his birthday surprise that I nearly blurted it out!

Unfortunately, the older I get, the more I realize I've gotten really good at *lying to myself*. And the older I get, the more I realize that the people around me don't want me to be perfect; they want me to be honest. They need me to acknowledge my feelings and take responsibility for them.

Here's a simple example. While visiting a city where a friend lives, I didn't get the opportunity to meet up with them. At first, I felt guilty and worried that this friend would be angry with me. I didn't know how to tell them that I was sorry, and

I was tempted to emotionally withdraw to avoid conflict. But the more I considered what I was feeling, and the more I was honest with myself, the more I realized that *I* was the one who was disappointed. With this shift in mindset, I could approach the relationship from a place of vulnerability. I could share how much I wanted to see that person and how sad I was that it didn't work out. I took control of my own emotions rather than trying to manage theirs.

It's easier for me to feel the disappointment of others—it feels more valid. But when I realize that my emotions matter, I find it safe to name and own the ones I experience.

Much like needing time to consider what I need help with, I need to take time to discover my emotions. For me, that means journaling or talking with a safe friend who loves me no matter what. It also means listening to others' stories and remembering that everyone has his or her own experiences. As much as I value honesty in others, I want to be honest with myself.

SHIFT IN FOCUS

What are some practices you can implement in your daily life to give you space to name and own your feelings? Is there anything you need to believe about God and yourself in order to do so?

During this last week, give yourself some time to write down or pray through what you have been learning during these sixty days.

Here are some sample journaling questions:

- Is there anything I've read about myself over the past week that felt hard to acknowledge?

- Which topic connected with me the most?

- Which topic encouraged me the most?

- What is one small step toward growth I can take today?

• • • • • • • • • • • • DAY 55

Growing in the Love of Beauty
By Christine Rollings

Be still, and know that I am God. I will be exalted among the
nations, I will be exalted in the earth!
(Psalm 46:10)

Dear Two, take a deep breath. Right now, as you hold this book, close your eyes and listen. What sounds do you hear around you? Name them. Write them down. What do you smell? Open your eyes. What movement do you see?

As I sit here and write, I hear cars driving by. I hear my husband in the kitchen, and I hear our dog's nails clicking on the hardwood floor. I smell coal in the air from people heating their homes. I see a stillness in my living room and out the window. There are dogs playing in the street and people walking, bags in hand, to the weekly farmers' market.

There is beauty everywhere. It can be simple, still, quiet, and ready for us to find with eyes of daily wonder.

Going to a Four and learning to grow in their best attributes means looking at the best of Fours for what we can learn. Fours have a natural radar for beauty, and many of them share that gift with the world through music, literature, and art. These people see beauty, make beauty, and show beauty. They reveal to us God's goodness in the world. As Twos, we can learn from this. We can also learn to slow down and savor.

When our identity no longer comes from what we do, how we help, or the appreciation we get, we no longer need to help constantly in order to live well. When we know deep in our soul that we are loved just for who we are and not for what we do or how much we give, we can sit back and rest in the truth that God reveals His beauty in everyday ways in this world.

What brings you delight? What gives you a sense of wonder? What makes you come alive?

For me, it can be the simple task of brewing a cup of coffee. I used to love the efficiency and speed of quick coffee, instant or from a pod. But lately, it has become a part of my morning ritual to make my coffee slowly: heat the water, measure and grind the beans, warm my cup, brew my coffee. And while sometimes this happens while I'm holding my baby or feeding my dog. It's still the reminder to slow down and savor this beverage that I've put care into making.

What about you? What do you want to slow down and savor in your life?

SHIFT IN FOCUS

Consider these questions for a moment. Use them to journal if that's helpful for you.

- What brings you delight? What gives you a sense of wonder? What makes you come alive?

- What is one practice you can add to your day that will fill you with simple beauty?

• • • • • • • • • • • DAY 56

Growing in Self-Care
By Christine Rollings

And he [Jesus] said to him, "You shall love the Lord your God with
all your heart and with all your soul and with all your mind.
This is the great and first commandment. And a second is like it:
You shall love your neighbor as yourself."
(Matthew 22:37–39)

You matter, dear Two. You are not here just to help others. You do not exist to serve. Without doing anything worthy of praise or gratitude, you are worthy of love simply for being here in this world.

You don't need special permission to take care of yourself. You don't need to have accomplished a certain number of tasks, answered a certain number of messages, or served a certain number of people in order to take care of yourself. You don't even need someone else to tell you that you can take care of yourself. Even so, I'm going to tell you, dear Two, that this is a beautiful area in which you can grow.

I've heard it said, and have even said it myself, that we need to take care of ourselves in order to better love and serve others. But I want to take a step back and say this: we need to take care of ourselves because it honors God. Our worth is not dependent on other people or how we serve them; our worth is dependent on God and who He says that we are.

When you take care of yourself, you love God with your heart, soul, and mind, taking care of His creation—you!

What does that look like for you in this season? It may be as simple as committing to eat three meals a day! I've been so busy at times, so consumed with what I've been doing, that I forget to feed myself! Feeding myself is self-care.

It's easy to jump right into tasks during the day, without taking the time you need to slow your heart. Maybe slowing your heart is as easy as making yourself a cup of tea or coffee or sitting down for a few minutes to journal or read before you begin each day. Giving yourself time for a restful start is self-care.

When you say no to things that aren't yours to do, when you ask for help from a friend or your spouse, when you accept love without earning it first—all of this, dear Two, is self-care.

Self-care doesn't mean you're self-absorbed. It doesn't mean you're selfish. Taking care of yourself can be a way to love God.

SHIFT IN FOCUS

Going to Four in growth means being honest with yourself about what you need to do to take care of yourself. Whether you are in a season of growth, a season of stress, or somewhere in between, you can take time now to think about what self-care means for you. Consider what you can do to take care of yourself emotionally, mentally, physically, and spiritually, and write these thoughts below.

Emotional	Mental	Physical	Spiritual
Example: *Journal*	*Example:* *Read a book*	*Example:* *Take a leisurely bath once a week*	*Example:* *Go to church without volunteering for anything*

DAY 57 • • • • • • • • • • •

Growing in Space-Saving: Don't Fix, Listen
By Christine Rollings

Know this, my beloved brothers: let every person be quick to hear, slow to speak, slow to anger.
(James 1:19)

The first time I mentored someone was in college. I was preparing to graduate, and my professor asked me to mentor a first-year student in the same program. She had just moved back to the United States for college, having spent most of her years in Europe, where her parents served as missionaries.

What do I have to offer her? I have never lived overseas, I thought to myself. Sure, I'd taught English in Europe for a few summers, but I quickly realized that I was in over my head when I met with her. Week after week, I listened, nodding along as I ate my college cafeteria lunch. I felt inadequate and unhelpful. I had no advice and could offer no help. But something happened a few months in—she told me how helpful I was, how much she looked forward to the time we spent together. Confused, I asked her to tell me more. "I just needed someone to listen. I needed to be able to tell my own story, to have someone hear me."

There was nothing to fix. She didn't need advice. She needed someone to be present, to save space for her to be herself and own her own story.

You know what space-saving feels like because you know exactly what it feels like when it isn't there. After you've poured your heart out, it's the half-hearted response "It will be okay" or "Just try harder next time" or even "God doesn't give us more than we can handle." It's the friend who tries to fix the problem rather than listen to it. The parent who jumps in with a solution when all you wanted was someone to hear you.

People want something to say. We Twos want to help people by listening. We want to take in all the information and respond with a solution that will not only fix the problem but also help our friend feel heard and loved.

Growing in space-saving requires growth in:

+ Emotional honesty: When we're honest with our own hearts and can acknowledge and take ownership of our own feelings, we can allow others to do the same.

+ The love of beauty: We need to slow down our hearts enough to listen and to sit in the in-between of what is being said.

+ Self-care: When we listen to others, it can be easy to take on their emotions and carry their burden. This kind of empathy seems helpful, but it is not our weight to bear. When we take care of ourselves and know our own limits and boundaries, we can be fully present for others as they carry their load.

Space-saving is one of the positive traits of type Fours. Sitting with others, feeling with them, and fixing nothing. This may feel very counterproductive at times, but the more you listen and save space for others to fully process and feel their emotions, the more you'll grow.

SHIFT IN FOCUS

Can you think of a time that someone saved space for you? How did you feel when they did? Pay attention today to your responses as others share. Are you quick to offer a solution? Are you able to listen without trying to make the person feel better? Instead of rushing to offer help, ask a follow-up question. Listen more attentively and offer your presence before your advice.

● ● ● ● ● ● ● ● ● ● ● ● **DAY 58**

Finding Your Creative Space

By faith we understand that the universe was created by the word of God, so that what is seen was not made out of things that are visible.
(Hebrews 11:3)

Creativity is one of the ways Twos go to Four in growth. You probably enjoy doing something creative, even if you don't classify it that way.

Do you sew, crochet, or knit?

Do you draw, paint, or watercolor?

Do you rearrange rooms or enjoy decorating?

Do you play an instrument or sing?

Do you cook or bake?

Do you write?

Now, you don't have to be good at any of these things to enjoy them. I think we all have a hard time creating because it can feel like a waste of time or a waste of materials, but it's only wasteful when you view it that way. You can glorify our creative God by creating, even if what you create is not a masterpiece or something to be praised. Amen?

If you're plagued by the idea of wastefulness, you can always create to give. Did you know that some hospitals accept homemade pillowcases for children while they're in for treatment? Make some and donate them. Watercolor blank pieces of paper to use as cards later. Create sugar scrubs at home and package them as holiday gifts that everyone loves.

All of these things give you permission to create, which is healthy for you! You need a creative outlet to grow in emotional honesty and empathy, and for your overall health. Prioritize creative pursuits. The best part is that you don't need to stick to one form of creativity. Pinterest and YouTube are great resources to teach you new skills and keep your creative spirit flowing. If you're bored with your current mode of creating, or have already gifted everyone in your circle with certain things, take up something new.

SHIFT IN FOCUS

Is there something you can create to give?

What creative outlet have you always wanted to try?

What would it look like to prioritize creativity?

• • • • • • • • • • • DAY 59

The Emotionally Aware and Honest Two

> *Put on then, as God's chosen ones, holy and beloved,*
> *compassionate hearts, kindness, humility, meekness, and patience,*
> *bearing with one another and, if one has a complaint against*
> *another, forgiving each other; as the Lord has forgiven you,*
> *so you also must forgive.*
> (Colossians 3:12–13)

A couple of positive traits Twos gain as they go to Four in growth are emotional awareness and emotional honesty. These two traits go hand in hand; you cannot honestly express your emotions if you do not first know what they are.

Emotional awareness might not feel like a gift when emotions are loud and unpleasant, but as any counselor would tell you, repressing your emotions (which feels more comfortable in the moment) is not a healthy way to process life.

Repressed emotions end up coming out sideways through manipulation, passive aggression, and other destructive behaviors. This is because we aren't actually dealing with these emotions; we're just shoving them down and hoping they stay put.

Emotional awareness looks like having hurt feelings and feeling the sting. Just like physical wounds, this pain is meant to prompt action. The pain from a burn compels you to move your finger away from a hot pot handle. Emotional pain is meant to lead you to reconciliation.

When pain feels suffocating, you have to do something about it. This may feel really upsetting when you're used to repressing such feelings.

This is where emotional honesty comes in.

What is emotional honesty? It's processing and expressing your true feelings. This can include repenting of how those feelings have impacted others in unkind ways, telling people how they have hurt you to make room for reconciliation, or honestly telling others what you want so they have the tools to love you well. Emotional honesty is not living in your feelings but rather working through them with an honest view of yourself, God, and all other parties.

You cannot be honest if you are repressing your true feelings, even if it's to please others. You can't please everyone, and if you try to do so, this phoniness sometimes takes the shape of bowing to others' sinful nature. People want you to be a certain way to please their need for control or comfort. It is not God-honoring to bow to other people's sin, and in turn sin yourself by lying about your intentions, emotions, and identity.

Perhaps you're in a season of growth. As you exercise emotional awareness and honesty, you'll learn that your feelings *do* matter, and you'll be more confident in relational problem-solving. You'll also become more secure in who you are and why you matter, as you find your identity in Christ.

This is what healthy Twos look like. They serve and keep their boundaries. They live loved, like their feelings matter—because they do. And they do not bow to others but champion them.

SHIFT IN FOCUS

Are you having any unpleasant emotions right now that may indicate some action you need to take?

Pick up your Bible and turn to any Psalm. Write down four emotions that it honestly expresses:

_____

_____

Isn't it awesome that God devoted an entire book of the Bible to the processing of emotions? If nothing else, this should show us how much God values our emotions. Notice in the Psalms how David vents, processes, and always ends with praise. This is what our emotions can look like when we process them with God. They present an opportunity for growth, loosening our grip on control and humbling ourselves before God.

DAY 60 • • • • • • • • • • •

The Best of You in Action

Practice these things, immerse yourself in them,
so that all may see your progress.
(1 Timothy 4:15)

Practicing new growth techniques as a Two can feel scary at first. You have to believe the opposite of everything shame has ever told you in order to ask for help, express your needs, and be emotionally honest. Taking action that says, "God, I agree with You about my worth" is terrifying when we don't fully believe that statement. It's okay for this to feel scary, bad, or almost impossible. God will help you.

Every time you take an action that says, "God, I agree with You about my worth" and everything turns out fine, then your needs are met. You're building up proof that shame has been sorely mistaken about your value all along. The more you embrace the things you gain from type Four, and let go of the chains of an identity rooted in others, the more you'll be able to live boldly and purposefully.

Satan is all about stopping your growth from coming into fruition. I wouldn't be surprised if you even noticed elements of spiritual attack as you prioritize growth...but that doesn't mean that growth isn't God's desire for you.

Going to Four in growth might, in fact, ruffle some feathers, not because it's bad, but because some people may be used to you repressing your needs and feelings. Honestly, this was probably more convenient for them.

People who actually love you and who want the best for you will champion you as you grow and transform. They'll recognize that this person whose voice they're now hearing was always there. They won't feel like they're losing you, just getting to know you better. These people are a gift.

Taking action steps that bring real growth may feel like jumping off a cliff because you're trusting God for the outcome. You're trusting that obedience is better than complacency. You're trusting what God said when He made you an equal with everyone else. As a child at the edge of a pool who jumps into his father's arms, you're trusting that God is ready to catch you.

SHIFT IN FOCUS

Use 1 Timothy 4:15 as a guideline for action.

"Practice these things."

You needed to practice every new skill you've ever learned. Growing as a Two is no different. Slowing down, finding your creative space, letting your emotions stay for a while, and listening to what they have to say may look like a dozen little steps, small victories that only you and God may notice. Don't be afraid to adopt the mindset of practice. Your growth journey won't always be giant leaps ahead for the rest of your life.

"Immerse yourself in them."

Over the last sixty days, which verse really spoke to you? I would encourage you to memorize it, write it down, and hang it somewhere you will see it. Immerse yourself in the truth of your worth in Christ, and you'll find yourself slowly but surely believing it to be true. If you haven't been a Christian for very long, or if you aren't in the habit of reading your Bible, this would be the time to start. Believing what God says about your worth is key to your growth, and you can't believe what He says without *knowing* what He says.

"So that all may see your progress."

Pick a couple of people in your life with whom to share your big or small victories. I hope a couple of people come to mind right away, but if they don't, there are plenty of Instagram or Facebook pages for Twos who would love to cheer you on in your wins. Be bold and share your wins as something worth celebrating. Let your brothers and sisters who have gone before you encourage you on this journey. Thank you for letting me share part of it with you!

Book Recommendations for Twos

Heather Holleman, *Seated with Christ: Living Freely in a Culture of Comparison* (Chicago, IL: Moody Publishers, 2015)

Dr. Henry Cloud and Dr. John Townsend, *Boundaries: When to Say Yes, How to Saw No to Take Control of Your Life* (Grand Rapids, MI: Zondervan, 1992)

Ann Voskamp, *One Thousand Gifts: A Dare to Live Fully Right Where You Are* (Grand Rapids, MI: Zondervan, 2010)

Rebecca K. Reynolds, *Courage, Dear Heart: Letters to a Weary World* (Carol Stream, IL: Tyndale House Publishers, 2018)

Steve Corbett and Brian Fikkert, *When Helping Hurts: Alleviating Poverty Without Hurting the Poor and Yourself* (Chicago, IL: Moody Publishers, 2009)

Brené Brown, *I Thought It Was Just Me (But It Isn't)* (New York, NY: Penguin Group USA, 2007)

Ruth Haley Barton, *Sacred Rhythms: Arranging Our Lives for Spiritual Transformation* (Downers Grove, IL: InterVarsity Press, 2006)

As the Enneagram has passed through many hands, and been taught by various wonderful people, I want to acknowledge that none of the concepts or ideas of the Enneagram have been created by me. I'd like to give thanks to the Enneagram teachers and pioneers who have gone before me, and whose work has influenced this devotional:

Suzanne Stabile

Ian Morgan Cron

Father Richard Rhor

Don Richard Riso

Russ Hudson

Beatrice Chestnut

Beth McCord

Ginger Lapid-Bogda

About the Author

Elisabeth Bennett first discovered the Enneagram in the summer of 2017 and immediately realized how life-changing this tool could be. She set out to absorb all she could about this ancient personality typology, including a twelve-week Enneagram Certification course taught by Beth McCord, who has studied the Enneagram for more than twenty-five years.

Elisabeth started her own Enneagram Instagram account (@Enneagram.Life) in 2018, which has grown to nearly 65,000 followers. Since becoming a certified Enneagram coach, Elisabeth has conducted more than one hundred one-on-one coaching sessions to help her clients find their type and apply the Enneagram to their lives for personal and spiritual growth. She has also conducted staff/team building sessions for businesses and high school students.

Elisabeth has lived in beautiful Washington State her entire life and now has the joy of raising her own children there with her husband, Peter.

To contact Elisabeth, please visit:

www.elisabethbennettenneagram.com

www.instagram.com/enneagram.life